Praise for The *In*

"This book is a one-stop-shop for teachers, administrators, special educators, and parents. Packed with comprehensive information and practical tips, Stephanie has made the IEP process understandable from start to finish. As a dad to a college student with dyslexia, dysgraphia, and dyscalculia, this is the book I wish I had when he started his journey."

—**Dan Jordan, LPC NCC CCTP,** Accessing College, former College Accessibility Coordinator

"Stephanie nailed it: writing IEPs is a task, but it's also an opportunity; it's a process, but it's also a promise; and it's tough, but she makes it easy! Teachers who love their students and want the best for them should master writing effective IEPs, and *The Intentional IEP: A Team Approach to Better Outcomes for Students and Their Families* provides the perfect guide to make the best out of every IEP!"

—**Timothy Kretchman,** Founder and Educational Strategist for Action Driven Education

"*The Intentional IEP* simplifies and streamlines the overwhelming process of creating an IEP. This book provides practical and functional tips for every step of the IEP process for a special education teacher."

—**Sasha Long, MA BCBA,** Founder and President of The Autism Helper, Inc.

The Intentional IEP

The Intentional IEP

IEP

A Team Approach to Better Outcomes for Students and Their Families

Stephanie DeLussey

JB JOSSEY-BASS™
A Wiley Brand

Published by John Wiley & Sons, Inc., Hoboken, New Jersey.
Published simultaneously in Canada.

For general information on our other products and services or for technical support,
please contact our Customer Care Department within the United States at (800) 762-
2974, outside the United States at (317) 572-3993 or fax (317) 572-4002.

Wiley also publishes its books in a variety of electronic formats. Some content that
appears in print may not be available in electronic formats. For more information
about Wiley products, visit our web site at www.wiley.com.

Library of Congress Cataloging-in-Publication Data is Available:

ISBN 9781394184729 (Paperback)
ISBN 9781394184736 (ePDF)
ISBN 9781394184743 (ePub)

Cover Design: Wiley
Cover Images: © kool99/Getty Images

SKY10061505_113023

Contents

Introduction

I have dreamed of being a teacher ever since I can remember. In elementary school, I would take extra copies of worksheets home and teach invisible students in my classroom, which was my bedroom. I'd save my babysitting money to buy Vis-á-Vis markers and clear shelf-contact paper to make transparencies for my overhead projector, which was my dresser. In high school, I tried to start an email chain with friends to add math word problems and forward them. While wildly unsuccessful at the email chain, I have always known I wanted to teach.

Special education came into my life when I was a teenager. I vividly remember going to Walmart with my mom and seeing someone she knew there. I remember hearing them talk about this person's younger son having a disability and needing extra help in school. I had no idea what any of it meant, but this is my very first memory of me knowing that being a special education teacher is what I was put on this Earth to do.

My senior project was all about No Child Left Behind, and after graduating high school, I went on to pursue a dual certification degree in Special Education N–12 and Elementary Education K–6 from Kutztown University of Pennsylvania. And in 2010, I graduated with my Bachelor's Degree and started to pursue my dream as a classroom special education teacher. It is true what they say though: nothing prepares you for teaching in the classroom quite like actually teaching in a classroom does.

No more than a month fresh out of college, I taught Extended School Year (ESY) through a local Intermediate Unit. My class was a severe autism unit, and honestly, I would not have survived that summer without the help of the paraprofessionals in the room with me. About a month after the end of ESY, I moved to northern Virginia and became a 7th-grade math co-teacher. The staff I worked with was incredible, administration was so supportive, the school was recently remodeled, and my caseload had about 20 students on it. Talk about a dream job! I loved this school and all of the students I worked with. I even got to write my first Manifestation Determination and Behavior Plan that year! At the end of that school year I remember thinking, "Steph, you made it through this school year! You can make it through anything!" It wasn't tough, but it was not what college had prepared me for—even though I loved every minute of it.

At the end of that school year, I jumped right back into teaching ESY. You know those things that non-teachers always say we're so lucky to have . . . there was no summer break for me my first four years of teaching. I lived and breathed being a teacher.

After my first year in Virginia, I moved back to Pennsylvania to be with my now-husband outside of Philadelphia. I struggled finding a teaching position for months, and this is when I started selling lessons I had created on www.teacherspayteachers.com. A few months later, I accepted a position as a K–8 resource teacher at a charter school in Wilmington, Delaware. The commute was rough, my caseload was enormous, but I was back in the classroom and I was going to make a difference. The staff and administration at this charter school were unmatched. And I mean, I actually wanted to go to the staff meetings because the people I worked with were so passionate about education. It was contagious. I worked at this charter school for a few months until a position as a high school instructional support team (IST) facilitator at a public school opened up. At this same time, I was working on my Master's Degree in Curriculum and Instruction and English as a Second Language because I wanted to help write curriculum and saw this new position as a next step.

As an IST facilitator, I worked closely with the general education teachers and administrators to identify and help students who didn't qualify for special education services, but needed additional supports. Through this position, I got to see the other side of special education. The side where staff and parents, sometimes together and sometimes not, were advocating for students and trying to find loopholes to get supports for these students who didn't qualify for special education services. Teacher me thrived in this position until the budget cut it a year and a half later.

Months later, I was hired by another charter school in Chester, Pennsylvania, to be a 5th-grade resource teacher. It wasn't long after this that we found out we were moving to Houston, Texas. We were thrilled, and as soon as we found out, I began transferring my teaching certifications to Texas. Within two months of being in Texas, I officially accepted a position as a grade 1–4 life skills teacher. I spent the entire summer getting ready, and as soon as I was allowed in my classroom to set up, I was there. I instantly fell in love with my class. We got to cook in the classroom, practice life skills, play to build motor skills . . . this classroom setting lit my teacher soul on fire. The next school year, I became the special education team leader in the building, and my caseload was exhausting, but I lived for it.

This was the first year I remember crying in an IEP meeting; I cared so much about my students and felt like no one at my school was listening to me when I advocated for the services my students deserved. You know how some years you teach, and other years teach you? My second year in life skills taught me. That class had so many needs, and on top of the day to day, I had to prove to the district that I desperately needed an additional paraprofessional.

Needless to say, I became that squeaky wheel advocating for my students, which turned into a very unhealthy and toxic situation the following school year.

Ultimately, I decided to leave the classroom mid-year.

It was the hardest decision I have ever made, to this day. I felt broken beyond repair, and I was ashamed and disappointed in myself that I left. The guilt ate me alive, and without being in a classroom, my entire identity of being a teacher shattered. At this same time, I was diagnosed with severe anxiety and PTSD. The following year was a blur of ignoring my mental health, until I finally decided to go to therapy and get help. There was always this little voice inside my head, though, that told me I needed to be in the classroom, so I went on interviews and would have anxiety attacks when offered the position. After experiencing the same phenomenon three times, I started listening to my body and what it was trying to tell me. I challenged myself to find my place in education that did not involve an actual classroom.

My journey in education has always challenged the traditional status quo of what being a teacher is and looks like. You know, the one where you teach in one classroom for 35 years and then retire. Fortunately, and unfortunately at the same time, education has changed a lot in the last decade. What I do see from the outside of the classroom setting is teachers setting harder boundaries than before, teachers taking back their worth and standing up to challenge the current state of education, and I see more students than ever being referred to special education, with teachers being given little to no guidance or training.

Flash forward a few summers—I was creating a resource to help teachers with IEP writing. I remember talking to one of my friends and she could see the light return in my eyes as I described this new resource to her. That conversation inspired me to dive deeper into what I love—IEP writing. One fun fact about me is I truly enjoy writing IEPs; I always have. The paperwork excites me and I could look at data for days, and I know I'm in the minority with this. That's when I came up with the idea for *The Intentional IEP*.

Since then, I have helped more than 30,000 teachers with their IEP writing through virtual and in-person trainings and I am proud to call myself an IEP Coach.

One thing that has always rung true for me as a veteran special education teacher is my love of students. To this day, everything I do is to make an impact in special education. To make positive waves in special education. To help you, the special education case-load manager.

Habit Building

IEP writing wasn't always easy for me. I committed many of the ultimate no-nos of IEP writing during my first years as a teacher:

- I spent nights writing IEPs at home.
- I wrote IEPs the night before the IEP meeting.
- I have not used data to make decisions.
- I have not always done my best to be collaborative and inclusive of the families I serviced.

I had a mentor teacher my very first year teaching, and the rest was on me to figure out—across multiple states, multiple classroom settings, and multiple IEP writing systems. The biggest lesson I had to learn had nothing to do with the process of IEP writing; I had to learn how to prioritize all the to-dos in my classroom, and it wasn't until my 5th year of teaching that I realized the importance of prioritizing my teacher job duties and responsibilities. I had to learn how to say "no" and I needed to break bad habits and build new habits because I needed to set boundaries to protect my mental health.

Before you continue through this book, I invite you to join me in an activity. This activity is the exact habit builder that I created and began using in my own classroom, and my hope is that by completing this quick 30-minute activity, you will be set on the pathway to becoming a stronger, more efficient IEP writer and advocate for your students.

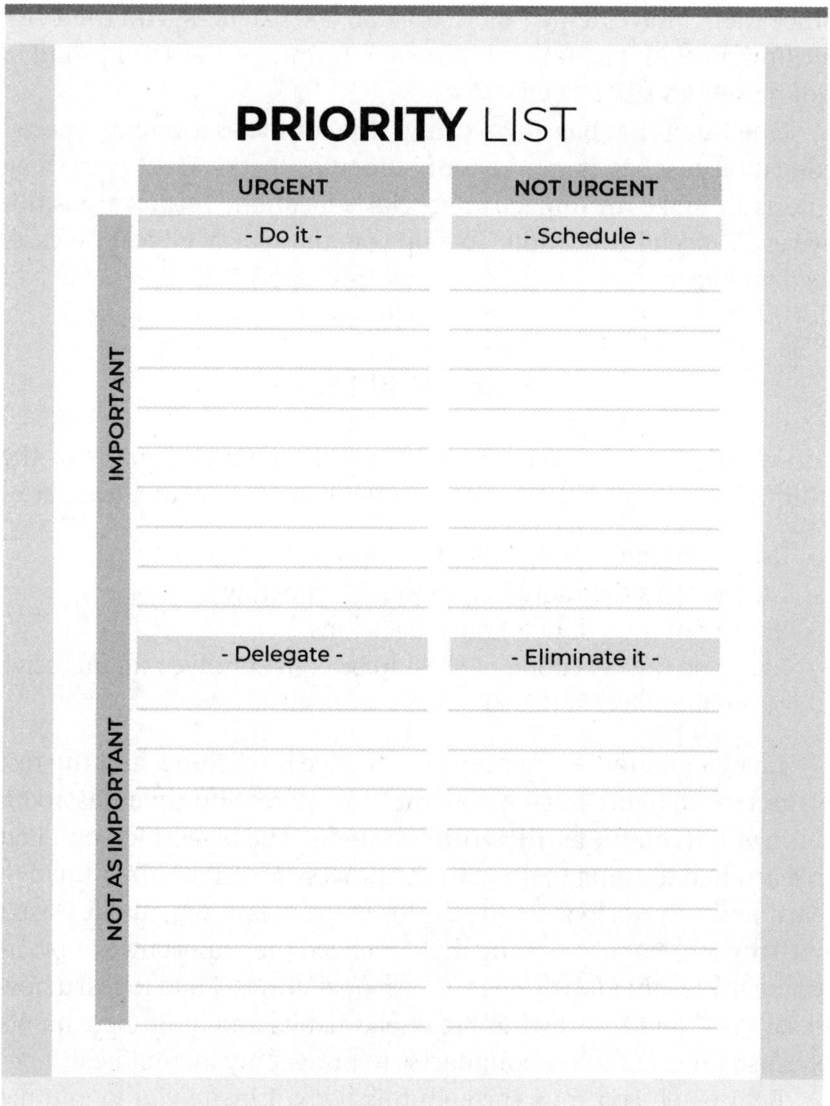

PRIORITY LIST

	URGENT	NOT URGENT
IMPORTANT	- Do it -	- Schedule -
NOT AS IMPORTANT	- Delegate -	- Eliminate it -

Figure I.1 Setting Your Priorities Will Help Organize Your Task and Goals

SOURCE: (c) Adobe Stock Images

You can visit the appendix of this book for blank templates for this activity.

Step 1: Brain Dump

On a blank piece of paper, you need to write down all of your mental notes and to-dos. Everything and anything, nothing is too big or too small to be written down. All of these things need to be out of your head so you have the mental capacity to show up for your students and yourself.

Tip: This step can be done all at once in one sitting, or accumulated across days. For example, I am the queen of sticky notes. My desk never has less than a dozen sticky notes with different things I need to do scribbled on them because if I don't write it down, I will forget it and it won't get done. It might be a chaotic brain dump, but I will let the sticky notes accumulate for no more than one week, and then I will do a quick brain dump and add my sticky notes to the paper.

Step 2: Break It Down

Remember how I said to write everything down, nothing is too big or too small? It's still true, but this is the part where you will break down the larger tasks into smaller tasks. Kind of like a task analysis, but maybe not as specific. You can do this on the same sheet of paper, or a separate one if you'd like.

Example: Let's say I have "lesson plan for math for week 26" as a to-do. This task breakdown might look like four different tasks: (1) determine which math skills will be taught during week 26, (2) determine the sequence of skills to be taught each day of the week, (3) determine what and how to teach each lesson each day of the week, and (4) determine how to assess the skill at the end of the week.

The most important point to remember about this step is that it will look different for each task and for each teacher. There's no right or wrong way here!

Step 3: Prioritize

This is the fun part because it's time to prioritize each of the tasks from your brain dump into one of three sections: Must Do, Do Later, Maybe Do.

- **Must Do**—These are tasks on your list that need to be completed. These tasks are generally time-sensitive, are student-specific, or have another task waiting so there is no other option than to get done.
- **Do Later**—These are tasks on your list that need to be completed, but not right now. The tasks have no immediate urgency and can wait a couple days or weeks to be completed.
- **Maybe Do**—These are tasks on your list that you'd like to get done, but may be tasks that don't actually need to be done. These tasks are not aligned to student achievement or your success as a teacher.

Remember: your priorities are unique to you, and there is no right or wrong!

Step 4: Your Big Three

Once you have your priorities organized into three separate lists, it's time to make your weekly task list. Each day should have no more than three big tasks on it that you need to or should complete. You can also use this method to set three big goals for the week.

Step 5: Revisit

As the week progresses, you may find that other things have popped up that have a higher priority than what you had planned on doing. Welcome to teaching, right? It's okay, and this is where your flexibility comes to the rescue.

You may also find that you completed your Big Three really quickly on a specific day of the week, and you have the time and mental capacity to handle another task from your priorities list.

You can then go back to your original list and select another task to complete that aligns with how you've prioritized your teaching duties and responsibilities.

As teachers, we always have a million and six things to do. And no matter what classroom setting you teach in, there will always be more to do. You can finish grading a stack of papers today, and tomorrow there will be another task waiting for you. Or you can decide to not laminate that center activity because going to your own child's sports event is more important. Truly, there's no quick fix to changing your habits. But, gradually, as you make a new habit here, let go of an old habit there, make another new habit here, you'll notice your system beginning to work for you and not against you. And you, my teacher friend, have just taken the first step into revamping your current system. Welcome! I'm so proud of you!

Chapter 1
IEP Rundown

Objective 1	Learner will glean information about the history of the federal IDEA law and how it came to be.
Objective 2	Learner will understand what an Individualized Education Program (IEP) is and how an individual may qualify for services.
Objective 3	Learner will discover the similarities and differences between IEPs and 504 Plans.

You are here reading this because you're a teacher or an Individualized Education Program (IEP) team member. That means you are providing a service to your students, more specifically, you are providing special education services that are mandated through federal and state laws.

The purpose of this chapter is to offer you background knowledge of the history of special education and what special education services are, with hopes that by understanding the reasons why these laws were enacted, you will better understand your role at a child's IEP meeting and in their education.

History of the Individuals with Disabilities Education Act

If we want to learn the history of special education services in schools, we have to go back before the Individuals with Disabilities Education Act (IDEA) was enacted. The fate of many individuals with disabilities prior to the 1950s and 1960s was many were shunned or institutionalized, of which the majority in institutions were placed in severely restrictive settings. These individuals were kept rather than taught or rehabilitated, and the families of these individuals had little to no say. More so—there weren't many resources available for families and individuals with disabilities to live at home, let alone attend school with their neighboring peers.

It wasn't really until the 1950s and 1960s that the federal government started to step in, passing the National Defense Education Act (PL 85-864). This was the first act obtained that gave federal funding for teachers to be trained to work with disabled children.

Many of these new practices and improved programs and services from the 1950s and 1960s laid the foundation for the future . . . or the services that are available today.

Here are some of the wave-making acts from during this time that helped pave the way for today's services:

- Training of Professional Personnel Act of 1959: Helped train educational leaders on how to educate children with disabilities.
- Mental Retardation Facilities and Community Mental Health Centers Construction Act of 1963:[1] Provision for funding of construction on facilities related to the prevention, care, and treatment of disabled individuals.
- Elementary and Secondary Education Act of 1965 (which is now Every Student Succeeds Act [ESSA] of 2015): The start of state provided grants.
- Economic Opportunities Amendments of 1972, now known as Head Start.
- Handicapped Children's Early Education Assistance Act of 1968.
- Rehabilitation Act of 1973.

It's important to know where we came from so we can understand why we have the services, programs, and supports available today, and so we know what services, programs, and supports are available for our students when making IEP recommendations.

Moving into the 1970s, only about one in five[2] students with a disability were educated in schools. Much of this was because school districts were not legally required to educate disabled children, and there were many laws that prevented and prohibited disabled children from attending school altogether . . . until 1975.

In 1975, the United States saw the landmark development and signing of the Education for All Handicapped Children Act (EHA) (Public Law 94-142).

Signed by President Gerald Ford on November 29, 1975, the four purposes of the EHA were:

1. "To assure that all children with disabilities have available to them . . . a free appropriate public education (FAPE), which emphasizes special education and related services designed to meet their unique needs,
2. To assure that the rights of children with disabilities and their parents . . . are protected,
3. To assist States and localities to provide for the education of all children with disabilities, and
4. To assess and assure the effectiveness of efforts to educate all children with disabilities."[3]

After being signed into law, the EHA gave and guaranteed each student with a disability access to a FAPE. FAPE is pivotal to our purpose as special education teachers because all children deserve the opportunity to attend public schools and have a right to an education.

Not only was Public Law 94-142 the first to clearly define FAPE, it also:

- Required school districts to include the parents and guardians.
- Mandated IEPs for each student with a disability.
- Required placement in the Least Restrictive Environment (LRE).

- Ensured disabled students are given nondiscriminatory tests (think: native language and tests that take the disability into consideration).
- Required due process procedures be in place.

The EHA took the necessary steps to protect students with disabilities and their families, giving them the right to an equal, yet individualized, education, but it also provided support to the states to help them meet each student's individual needs.

In the 1980s and 1990s, there was a huge push for more opportunities for children with disabilities. Children in institutions were now being serviced under EHA and many were integrated with their nondisabled peers in public schools.

During this time we also saw:

- The U.S. Supreme Court address FAPE for the first time.
- More support for improved transition programs (think: vocational skills).
- Transition from high school to adult living.

In 1982, a landmark Supreme Court Case (*Board of Education v. Rowley*)[4] ruled that the law was to provide "a basic floor of opportunity to learn," as opposed to the achievement of maximum potential. It's important to remember this: FAPE is an opportunity as opposed to an unmeasurable outcome (i.e., maximum potential). The ruling also said that the state must provide sufficient supports and services to allow the child to benefit educationally from instruction, which you may now hear called "The Rowley Standard."

In 1984, in *Irving Independent School District v. Amber Tatro*,[5] the courts determined that if a service can be performed by someone other than a physician and the service does not involve a medical diagnosis or evaluation, the service is a "related service" and would be included in a child's IEP.

In 1988, in *Honig v. Doe*, the court ruled a disabled student may not be expelled "for an indiscriminate amount of time," and the student may not be suspended for more than 10 days at a time. During the temporary suspension, the IEP team may meet to determine a new placement. It also ruled that if the student's misconduct is related to the student's disability, an alternative placement should be considered instead of a suspension or expulsion. More changes to disciplinary procedures arose in 1997.

Another pivotal court proceeding in 1989, *Timothy vs. Rochester School District*, resulted in the Zero Reject principle. The Zero Reject principle is one of the core principles of IDEA that states that a child cannot be denied an education due to the severity of their disability.

During the 1976–1977 school year, the EHA serviced more than 3.5 million children with disabilities, aged 3–21. During the 1980–1981 school year, the number of students serviced increased to over 4 million. During the 1990–1991 school year, the IDEA serviced 4.7 million children with disabilities.[6]

In 1990, the EHA was reauthorized and became known as the Individuals with Disabilities Education Act (IDEA), or Public-Law 102-119.

There were three main amendments to the law in following years—1983, 1990, and 1997—that supported the transition initiatives, which lead to IEPs, including transition plans:

- Identifying appropriate employment and other post-school adult living objectives for the student.
- Referring the student to appropriate community agencies.
- Linking the student to available community resources, including job placement and other follow-up services.

Other notable changes in the 1997 amendment to IDEA were:

- An emphasis on a disabled child's access to the general education curriculum.
- Changes to disciplinary procedures.

The latter was due to an increase of student drug use and possession of dangerous weapons. The amendment outlined the following:

1. School personnel are allowed to change the placement of a disabled student in certain situations, such as possession of illegal drugs or weapons.
2. A change of placement to an interim setting or suspension must not be longer than 10 days.
3. A change of placement to an alternative educational setting may be considered, but only for the same amount of time that a non-disabled peer would be subject to the discipline, and not more than 45 days.
4. An interim alternative placement may only be considered when the child's current placement could cause harm to the student or others, the current placement is inappropriate, and the school has made an effort to minimize the current risk with supplementary aids and other services and supports.
5. If disciplinary action is required, a manifestation review is required.

In 1997, the amendments also restructured IDEA into four parts:

- Part A addresses general provisions.
- Part B covers assistance for education of all students with disabilities.
- Part C covers infants and toddlers with disabilities.
- Part D addresses national activities to improve the education of students with disabilities.

It's important to note that during this time too, Part H of the EHA was amended and changed to Part C of the IDEA. This is the section of the law that includes and helps states develop early intervention programs for infants and toddlers with disabilities. This section requires the development of Individualized Family Service Plans (IFSP) for each student, age birth to three.

All of these impactful revisions to the EHA and IDEA laws have helped you, as a special education teacher and IEP team member, better service your students to prepare them for further education, employment, and independent living. And all of these changes continue into the 2000s.

In 2004, the reauthorization of the IDEA aligned it with the No Child Left Behind Act requirements. This reauthorization and alignment called for:

- Early intervention for students
- Greater accountability and improved educational outcomes.
- Raised standards for instructors who teach special education classes.
- Requirement of the development of alternate standards.
- More specifics on the allocation and use of special education funds.[7]

In 2006, we also saw more revisions to the IDEA, including:

- Schools being required to use research-based interventions.
- What the resolution process looks like when a parent files a due process complaint.
- More details on how students in a private school are serviced.

In 2008, the law brought more clarity to parental consent, state monitoring, allocation of funds, and positive efforts for employment of individuals with disabilities.

The years of 2011, 2013, and 2015 (Every Student Succeeds Act) brought more revisions, and one of the most notable changes to the law was enacted in 2017 with Rosa's Law, which replaced the term *mental retardation* with *intellectual disability*.

All in all, during the 2018–2019 school year, over 7.5 million students with disabilities from birth to age 21 were serviced under the IDEA. When you compare those numbers to the 1950s, a time when students with disabilities were not receiving any services or supports, the fact that 66% of students with disabilities that are served in a general education classroom for at least part of the day is a huge cause for celebration.[8] There is still work to be done, but the historical path shows us moving in a positive direction.

IDEA Is Meant to Be Interpreted by Schools and Districts

When Congress enacted the IDEA, it placed more emphasis on the process rather than specifics. This means that it was left up to the schools and districts to make decisions too. For example, the IDEA tells us the rules for evaluating a child, but does not provide specific eligibility information for each disability category. These determinations are left up to the states to determine. While some states use wording verbatim from the IDEA, many parallel the law, but also add in their own requirements that provide greater protection and more rights for a child with a disability.

It's important to know that the laws, regulations, and policies by which you teach can change at any moment—as special education teachers are all too well aware of. You should familiarize yourself with your state's department of education website and the IDEA website, along with other notable special education websites like Wright's Law and The Intentional IEP.

Homework: Locate your state's Department of Education website and bookmark it. Then locate and bookmark the websites for the IDEA, Wright's Law, and The Intentional IEP.

What Is an IEP?

For the first time in history, with the 1975 signing of the Education for All Handicapped Children Act (EHA), schools experienced the legal obligation of each disabled child receiving an IEP. An IEP lays out the special instruction, services, and/or supports that a child with a disability will receive. IEPs act as a product that helps process and guide the instruction of students with disabilities.

In other words, an IEP is a legally bound document created by a team of professionals (and the child's parent or caregiver!) that work with a child who is experiencing struggles in school. But more than that, it's a map for a child's education program that includes special education instruction, services, and supports.

And similar to snowflakes and fingerprints, no two IEPs are the same, and no two IEPs *should* be the same. That's why the *I* in *IEP* stands for *individualized*.

Congress reauthorized the IDEA in 2004, and most recently, amended the IDEA through Public Law 114-95, also known as the Every Student Succeeds Act, in December 2015 . . . to which it says that an IEP is ". . . designed to meet [a student's] unique needs and prepare them for further education, employment, and independent living."

As a special education teacher and service provider, you know that an IEP is a legal document. And this goes without saying, but you also know that an IEP is not a recommendation or a suggestion. What's in the IEP *must* be provided to the student.

Who Can Have an IEP?

IEPs are a part of public education and are covered under the special education law IDEA. Any child with a disability, aged 3 to age 21, who attends a public school, inclusive of charter schools, is eligible for an IEP under the IDEA.

To qualify for special education services under the IDEA law, a child must meet two requirements:

- The child must be formally diagnosed with having a disability that is one of the 13 categories outlined in the federal law.

- The school must determine that, as a result of the disability, the child needs special education services to make progress in school and learn the general education curriculum.

Not all students who struggle in school qualify for special education services.

To determine eligibility, a child must go through the evaluation process and will be assessed by a qualified examiner, in school with an educational evaluation or through an outside Independent Educational Evaluation (IEE).

In schools, the initial evaluation may occur only if the parent or caregiver has given written permission. Once the request for evaluation is received and the parent or caregiver has provided consent for testing, the school entity has 60 days to conduct the evaluation, per IDEA regulations.

The evaluation includes formal tests, informal assessment measures, observations, interviews with multiple members on the team, and any other assessments deemed necessary. Comprehensive evaluations may include, but are not limited to:

- An individual psychological evaluation.
- Social history.
- Physical examination (think: specific assessments for vision, hearing, and health).
- Observation(s) of the student in their current educational setting.
- Educational evaluation.
- Vocational assessments at transition age.

Don't forget that any evaluations and assessments must be given to the student in their native language.

A child's parent or caregiver also has a right to ask for the IEE if they decide the evaluations recommended or completed by the school are not appropriate or sufficient. However, the district does not have to agree, at which time the district will initiate an impartial hearing. Either way, the IEP team is provided with the outside evaluation and determines if the information in the evaluation is permitted and/or sufficient for determining eligibility.

After the educational evaluation, the IEP Team, which includes the child's family, reviews the evaluation results and determines if the child is eligible to receive special education services.

It's important to mention that a doctor provides a diagnosis. Educators determine eligibility and cannot provide a diagnosis.

Again, to be eligible, the child must meet both eligibility criteria:

1. The child must have a disability that adversely affects their educational performance.
2. The school must determine that, as a result of the disability, the child needs special education services to make progress in school and learn the general education curriculum.

As previously mentioned, there are 13 disability categories outlined in the IDEA that may qualify a student for special education services. Think of the categories as doors that open a pathway to special education services.

The 13 categories are:

- Autism Spectrum Disorder.
- Deafness.
- Deaf-blindness.
- Emotional Disturbance.
- Hearing Impairment.
- Intellectual Disability.
- Orthopedic Impairment.
- Other Health Impairment.
- Specific Learning Disability.
- Speech or Language Impairment.

- Traumatic Brain Injury.
- Visual Impairment (including Blindness).
- Multiple Disabilities.

A child can be diagnosed with one or more than one disabilities. Typically, if a child is diagnosed with multiple disabilities, one of the diagnoses is determined the most prevalent, followed by the child's secondary disability, tertiary disability, and so on.

Did you know? During the 2020–2021 school year, 15% of students attending public schools required special education services under the federal law.[9]

Once a child is determined to be eligible for services, the IEP team writes the child's IEP. If the child is an infant from birth to 3 years old, the information is used to create the child's IFSP, which helps the child work toward meeting developmental milestones.

Other important things to note about IEPs:

- Students younger than age 3 can receive services through early intervention.
- Private schools do not offer IEPs, but students may still be able to receive services through what is called an Individual Service Plan.
- Students beyond age 21 do not receive services; however, students may still receive accommodations through disability services at the college level or at their place of work under the Americans with Disabilities Act (ADA), which provides individuals with disabilities freedom from discrimination at work.

Who Is on the IEP Team?

Each child's IEP team is different, and each member of the IEP team plays a vital role. An IEP team includes:

- The child's parent, guardian, or caregiver.
- One general education teacher.

- One special education teacher.
- A representative of the public agency (the Local Education Agency, or LEA).
- Someone who can interpret data.
- When appropriate, the student.

The IEP team may also consist of other individuals who have knowledge or expertise regarding the student, at the discretion of the parent or caregiver and the school district. These other persons may include related service providers, school social worker or guidance counselor, outside therapists, school physician, or others.

In elevated situations, you may also be in attendance of a lawyer or advocate at an IEP meeting, along with other higher-up school personnel.

Each member of the IEP team holds a different role, and their knowledge and expertise are highly needed at the IEP table. The following sections look at key team members and their roles and responsibilities as a vital part of the IEP team.

Parent, Guardian, or Caregiver

Parents are key members on the IEP team and are experts on the child. They can offer insights into the child's life outside of school, what works well at home and what doesn't, past or current struggles and victories, and so many other things that only a parent would know.

Parents should share their thoughts and concerns with the team and offer suggestions as well. They should report back to the IEP team with any changes noticed at home.

Special Education Teacher

The special education teacher is often the student's caseload manager. This individual is the special education expert on the team who has expertise on the child's disability and its impact on the student's development and educational progress. This teacher can provide insight on the long list of services and supports a child may benefit from, and they ensure that the services outlined in the child's IEP are being provided.

Typically, the special education teacher is the one who writes the IEP, collects data, and provides reporting information as outlined in the IEP. Other job duties vary depending on where a teacher works, including scheduling and running the IEP meeting and finalizing the IEP.

General Education Teacher

The general education teacher is a vital component of the IEP team. This person is a grade level content knowledge expert, and part of their role includes sharing academic expectations for the child's grade or a particular subject with the IEP team. This knowledge and expertise help the team establish goals and objectives for the child's IEP that directly relates to the grade level content standards and the child's same-aged, nondisabled peers.

General education teachers should help write the IEP by providing knowledge and suggestions. They should ask questions if help is needed, advocate for and attend professional development as needed, advocate for student needs in their classroom, work with and include the student in their classroom, accommodate and modify lessons and materials as needed, and collect data on appropriate goals and the use of services and supports in their classroom.

Local Education Agency (LEA)

The LEA must be qualified to provide or supervise the provision of instruction, must know about and be knowledgeable with the general education curriculum, and must be knowledgeable about the availability of resources the school can provide. This person also needs to be capable of authorizing school funds to provide necessary services within the student's IEP, and ensure the team that the services outlined in the child's IEP will be fulfilled.

Data Interpreter

This individual must be able to explain evaluation results to the team and interpret evaluation results to help design the child's IEP. If it is an evaluation year, this might be a diagnostician or other evaluator. Often times, this is a dual role with the child's special education teacher.

Student

According to the IDEA, a student reaches transition age at the age of 16. This age varies, and can be as early as age 12. This is when the student must be invited to their own IEP meetings and be a part of their educational plan. Students can participate in all or part of the meeting, as deemed applicable by team members, as participation is an important step in developing self-advocacy skills. Younger students may also participate, and you will learn more about student-led IEP meetings later in this chapter.

Transition services extend to age 21 and are a coordinated set of activities monitored by the school that are designed to prepare the student for adult life. I talk more about transition services in Chapter 3.

At the age of 18, a student is at the age of majority. This age varies state to state, and means that the parent or caregiver is no longer the key decision-maker. At this point, the student is transferred the rights to make educational decisions for themself. I talk more about this in Chapter 3 too.

The Art of Team Collaboration

It's also important to remember that each child's team has its own unique culture. How the meeting is structured, the complexity of the language and documents, the meeting room environment, the team's values . . . all of these nuances create the dance that is a truly collaborative IEP process. To begin this collaborative process, each team member must believe they are there for the student's benefit.

(continued)

(continued)

To read more specifics within the IDEA law on IEP team members, you can search for Section 300.321. Ultimately, IDEA defines the key players on the IEP team, but does not provide a roadmap for collaborative IEP team success. I discuss team collaboration more in Chapters 4 and 5.

What Does the IEP Team Do?

The IEP team meets to talk about the child's needs and write the student's IEP. Parents and the student—again, when appropriate—are a vital part of the IEP team. Parents hold valuable information that school professionals may not know or be aware of, and when parents feel like a valuable part of the IEP team, you can use this information to craft bigger success for the student.

When it comes to writing the IEP document, it really depends on what and how your school does this. The IEP writing process itself is not something that is outlined in IDEA, and you may find that three different schools may write IEPs the same exact way, or each a different way. It's important to note, too, that there is no one right or wrong way to write an IEP as long as the law, your state's regulations, and your school's policies are being followed.

Examples of different ways school teams write IEPs:

- Some schools write the IEP at the IEP meeting.
- Some schools hold an IEP meeting, discuss the IEP details, and write the IEP after the meeting.
- Some schools write portions of the IEP prior to the IEP meeting, and then discuss and make changes to the proposed IEP at the meeting.

In a perfect world, the entire IEP team would be writing the IEP at the meeting because all members of the IEP team are actively involved in writing the student's IEP. More importantly, parents feel like active, involved members of the IEP team when this occurs. This is not to say you cannot have a collaborative IEP writing process any other way; you can read more about collaboration in Chapters 4 and 5.

All of the schools I have worked in across multiple states and districts wrote the proposed IEP prior to the meeting and made changes at the meeting. When I polled IEP teams, I found that 90% write IEPs in this manner.

The Referral Process

It is important to know that any child may be referred for special education services and supports, but not all children who struggle will be determined eligible for services under the IDEA.

The referral process starts in one of two ways, through Child Find or with the parent or public agency making an initial referral.

Child Find is the process that school districts must follow to look for, find, and evaluate individuals who need special education services and supports, age birth to 21; it is also termed for students who are deemed "at risk." Both state and local education agencies, or schools, are given the responsibility by federal and state laws to conduct Child Find activities so that children who need special services have the opportunity to receive those services.

This obligation to identify all children who may need special education services exists even if the school is not providing special education services to the child, including children who attend private schools and public schools, highly mobile children, migrant children, homeless children, and children who are wards of the state.

Child Find is mandated by the IDEA and its purpose is:

- To promote public awareness of disabilities.
- To alert parents, professionals, and the public to children who may have a disability.

- To assist public agencies in finding children who may have disabilities and who otherwise may not have come to their attention.
- To enable children and families to receive the special education and related services that are needed.

Essentially, the Child Find mandate requires each state to devise a practical method to determine which children are receiving the needed special education services, and which children are not. This can be done through public outreach efforts, local media campaigns, public notices, and so on.

After identifying a student who may need special education services, the Child Study Team (CST) will make a referral for a comprehensive evaluation.

This means that an adult who works with the child is making an initial request for the child to be evaluated for special education.[10] This request can be done verbally or in writing, but I do recommend the request to be in writing and it should be dated.

This referral may also come from the Child Study Team.

As a parent or teacher who is advocating for something you believe a disabled child may need, I recommend always writing a letter and delivering it to the appropriate administrator, and date the document. You can then follow up via email or phone to check on the progress of the concerns outlined in the hand-delivered letter.

Once the written referral is received, the school has a specific number of days to respond to the request, which is outlined in the state's Procedural Safeguards. The school does not have to agree to a request for evaluation if they have no reason to believe the child has a disability that requires services. But if the public agency has reason to suspect a disability, they must evaluate the child. If the agency accepts the request, the school must conduct the initial evaluation within 60 days of receiving parental consent. The public agency may also recommend additional screening prior to a comprehensive evaluation.

If the public agency initiated the referral, it will be important to include any documentation and data collected prior to the referral request.

Also, if the public agency has initiated the request, not only must they immediately notify the parent or caregiver that the child has been referred for an evaluation, but they must also receive parental consent to move forward with the evaluation. Even if the parent has initiated the request, the parent must still sign the consent form for a full, comprehensive evaluation. Consent means that the parent has full knowledge of the district's actions, and the parent may request an informal meeting to discuss the referral in more depth.

The parent does not need to agree to the referral, but the public agency does have legal obligations to uphold. If the parent does not agree, the public agency will usually try to hold multiple meetings with the CST, administrators, and the IEP team. If no agreements can be made, parents and the public agency have due process rights to explore.

However, in most cases, parents do provide consent for full comprehensive evaluations. Evaluations are done at no cost to the parent or guardian, and all evaluations must be completed within 60 days of the consent to evaluate. After the evaluation is complete, the team will hold an eligibility meeting. Once a student has been determined eligible for special education services, the school has 30 days to write the IEP and hold the initial IEP meeting. (This is per IDEA. States and districts may use different timelines.) This means it's time to write the student's IEP.

For students eligible under the category of Developmental Delay, a reevaluation must be completed 30 days prior to the student's ninth birthday. The age requirement varies state to state.

The IEP Writing Timeline

Before you can begin writing a child's IEP, it is important to follow through with best practices and timelines to ensure IEP process effectiveness. This is where the IEP Writing Timeline, shown in Figure 1.1, becomes your new best friend.

The Best Time to Start

Believe it or not, starting an IEP 45 days from the date of the actual meeting is the best time to start. This gives you enough time to communicate and schedule with all the crucial stakeholders and team members, gather your data, write a quality IEP, ask for needed feedback, and be ready to present at the meeting.

Start by looking at the expiration date of the student's most recent IEP document, and then 45 days prior to this is the day to start. At the beginning of the school year, when you receive your caseload, determine the start date for all of your IEPs and add them to your calendar. This way you can begin the process at the right time for every student, no questions asked.

When you've reached your 45-day date, begin connecting with families and staff members to determine the meeting date. Be sure it is in compliance so the IEP doesn't expire before the meeting is held.

Once you have your IEP meeting date determined, send out formal invitations.

About 30 days out from your scheduled meeting, reach out to the team members (including general education teachers and student families) to gain input on the content of the IEP. This helps with communication and relationship building, as well as helps you get important insight and write the IEP.

Once you have this information, get writing! Spend the next week or two carving out time here and there to write the text-heavy sections of the IEP, like the Present Levels of Academic and Functional Performance.

IEP Writing Timeline

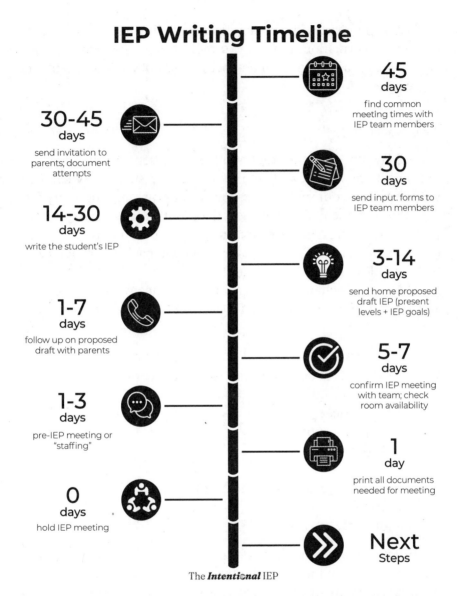

45 days find common meeting times with IEP team members

30-45 days send invitation to parents; document attempts

30 days send input. forms to IEP team members

14-30 days write the student's IEP

3-14 days send home proposed draft IEP (present levels + IEP goals)

1-7 days follow up on proposed draft with parents

5-7 days confirm IEP meeting with team; check room availability

1-3 days pre-IEP meeting or "staffing"

1 day print all documents needed for meeting

0 days hold IEP meeting

Next Steps

The *Intentional* IEP

Figure 1.1   The IEP Writing Timeline.

When you start with writing instead of clicking boxes or entering other information, it gives you more time to go back and edit later, when you have a fresh perspective and other team members at the table.

Anatomy of an IEP

An IEP lays out all of the student's needs and services, and depending on where you work (such as district or state) or what IEP writing system your school uses, your IEP format may look very different from the school or state next door. But all IEPs have common parts, or sections, and once you know what information goes into each section of an IEP, you'll be best suited to navigate through any transfer IEP you receive.

Later in this chapter, I dive deeper into the anatomy of an IEP and all of an IEP's sections, but for now, all IEPs must contain these parts:

- Student information.
- Present levels of academic and functional performance.
- Goals and objectives or benchmarks.
- Related services.
- Supplemental supports.
- Progress reporting.
- Testing.
- Least restrictive environment determination.
- Transition.
- Parental consent.

IEP documents can be tens of pages long, so keep in mind that these parts are not the only sections in a child's IEP.

Evaluations are performed at a minimum of every three years to determine whether the child is still in need of special education services. The parent or caregiver may request additional testing every year, once a year, but it is left up to the discretion of the school to provide additional testing on non-reevaluation years.

Subsequent evaluations, or reevaluations, are to be conducted every three years, but parents may request one evaluation per year under the IDEA. Schools can deny the additional testing each year, within guidelines under the IDEA. This is also where the Procedural Safeguards come into play for parent and student rights.

At a minimum, IEPs are reviewed annually, but changes and additional amendment meetings can take place at any time throughout the year, as requested by any individual on the IEP Team.

Once You've Written Parts of the IEP

When you are two weeks, or 14 days, away from the meeting date, send home a drafted IEP to the student's family. At a minimum, a proposed draft IEP should be sent three school days prior to the student's IEP meeting.

When you're one to seven days away from the big meeting date, depending on when you sent the proposed draft IEP home, reach back out to the family if you haven't heard from anyone yet. You will want some time to converse about their input as well as incorporate their feedback into the document as needed.

Now you're one step ahead for the upcoming IEP meeting!

Around five to seven days before the meeting, confirm the date with everyone. Many related service providers have very large caseloads, and things can get lost in translation. This is also the time to ensure you have a room ready for the meeting. Some schools require you to secure a room, while others have a room specifically for IEP meetings. Be sure you have a space to meet.

Who will be covering your classroom while you're in the IEP meeting? Check with your administration and/or school secretary to be sure there is coverage for your class if needed. Start ensuring you have work and a plan for this person to engage in with your class while you're in the meeting.

If I have learned anything in my years as a special educator, it's not to trust technology the day you need it, and always have a backup plan. So the day before the meeting, start printing needed documents (the IEP!). There are a lot of papers to sign and hard copies to hand out, so make sure all of the needed paperwork is printed and stapled.

Any data, student work, or informational handouts you want for the meeting should be gathered and organized so you have it all ready when you need the information in the meeting.

The IEP Meeting

All of your hard work and preparation over the last few weeks have led up to this day: the IEP meeting. Depending on where you work, you may or may not be the facilitator of the IEP meeting.

Types of IEP Meetings

Before you can learn about what to do at an IEP meeting, you need to know about the different types of IEP meetings.

Eligibility Meeting

The purpose of an eligibility meeting is to determine if the child qualifies for special education services. At this meeting, the IEP team will review all of the data, including testing and evaluation reports from the school and outside the school, to make a decision. If a child is found eligible for special education services, then that the team will develop the child's IEP.

Any determination made ahead of time is known as *predetermination* and is against the federal IDEA law. The decision needs to be made by the team at the eligibility meeting.

Remember that the parent must provide consent for an initial evaluation and any assessment or placement decision.

Initial IEP Meeting (and Initial Reviews)

An initial IEP meeting occurs when a child is first found eligible for special education services and the team begins writing the child's first IEP. This is the child's first IEP.

Holding the eligibility meeting and initial IEP meeting back-to-back may not be best practice for many IEP teams. Eligibility meetings are often information overload for families; this is unchartered waters for them and they are probably feeling a lot of different emotions. If you want the parents to be active participants in the IEP process, it is best practice to hold the initial IEP meeting on a separate day. You can read more about supporting parent participation in Chapter 5. This also allows other IEP team members to provide thoughtful input and data that is needed for making these important decisions.

Annual IEP Meeting

IEP meetings are required by IDEA law to happen a minimum of no less than once every calendar year. This meeting is generally called the annual IEP meeting, and its purpose is to provide the IEP team with the opportunity to discuss and analyze relevant data to make changes to the child's current IEP. This involves looking at the child's progress reports, grade reports, attendance, classroom work samples and test results, diagnostic test results, and so on to discuss current concerns and successes the team has noticed over the last year.

Student-Led IEP Meeting

Any child with special education services has IEP meetings, and in most cases, the child doesn't attend or have a say in the meeting until middle school, when transition services come into play. However, you may have noticed the positive trend in general education classrooms where students are leading parent-teacher conferences and taking ownership of their education. But what about our students with disabilities? Why aren't we preparing our students for taking owner-ship of their learning, education, and future when they are in ele-mentary school? Why are they not involved sooner, and what about our students who are nonverbal or moderately to severely disabled? How can we get them involved, and what does it even look like?

Many times teachers are left to translate student actions and approximations into data, which in turn becomes a progress update or a new IEP goal. And an IEP is the most important document any disabled child has in regard to further education, employment, and independent living. So why not give the student a chance to tell the IEP team what they want?

Involve the Student as Early as Appropriate

Research shows that when students participate in IEP meetings, they have greater self-advocacy skills, greater self-determination skills, better transition outcomes, and a higher quality of life. Hav-ing students involved at an earlier age is only going to increase that confidence and the student's communication and presentation skills as they move forward. There are many ways a student can be a part of the IEP meeting, regardless of disability or age. You know the transition age per the IDEA is age 16, but students should be involved in their IEPs before this age. So how do you do that? When students are younger, involvement might look like sharing informa-tion. What they like about school, what they feel like they are good at, what they like doing, something they'd like to learn or learn how to do, and so on.

As students get older, involvement can be more detailed and intentional in their IEP role. This might look like leading discus-sions about what the student feels has worked for them, helping the team plan for the student's future, determining goals for the stu-dent's IEP, and so on. Having students be a part of their IEP process comes down to student and parent buy-in. Both parties have to see and believe in the messaging and hype behind student-led IEPs and student-centered IEPs for them to be successful.

Before implementing student-led IEPs or teaching the student more about their own IEP or disability, it is best practice to have a conversation with the child's parents.

During the preparation phase, once an IEP meeting date has been agreed on by all adult parties, it all starts with an invitation to the IEP meeting—an invitation to the student and an invitation from the student. As the teacher, you can create an invitation to the student to ask them to attend or be a part of the IEP meeting.

In addition to the formal invitation sent home, have the student write or fill out a personalized invitation for team members. Depending on your student's age and disability, this might look very different. For younger students or students who need more support, this might look like a tracing activity of the student tracing the words on the invitation page or a cut-and-paste activity that fills in the blanks of when and where the meeting will take place. For older students or students who need less support, this might look like the student creating and writing the IEP invitation independently. Table 1.1 outlines some age-appropriate tasks that you can help students with so that they are an active part of the process.

Table 1.1 Age-Appropriate IEP Student Responsibilities

Elementary School	Middle School	High School
Help set goals	Help set goals	Help set goals
Share what works well in helping them learn	Fill out questionnaires and input forms	Fill out questionnaires and input forms
Share about friends	What inspires them	What inspires them
Share likes and dislikes and what inspires them	Help write Present Levels	Help write Present Levels
Share favorites (in and out of school)	Get ready for transition	Transition

As the child's teacher, I also recommend sending home a parent letter, letting the parent know that their child is working on a student portfolio that will be shown and discussed at the IEP meeting.

Prepare the Student Portfolio with the Student

During the waiting period between invitations and the actual meeting, you and the student will work on the student portfolio. Inside the student's portfolio might be:

- **Student questionnaire**: This input form will give the team information on the student's likes and dislikes, what goals the student wants to work toward, how the student feels about school and their classes, things the student feels good at or things they feel they need more help with, the student's vision statement, and other important information only the student can provide. Depending on student supports and age, the delivery method of this questionnaire may look different and will vary for each student on your caseload.

- **Interest inventory or self-assessments**: The purpose of these documents is to help you determine a student's strengths, preferences, and interests in relation to employment and job skills, continuing education and training, independent and supported living, community involvement, and recreation and leisure. While this may seem more appropriate for older students, remember that your younger students already have an idea in their head about what they want to be when they grow up, and even in elementary school we can prepare a student for further education, employment, and independent living. For example, if a younger student says they want to be a basketball player when they grow up, this may be the opportunity to get the student involved in the school or community's basketball program, teach the student about good sportsmanship and social skills for being a team player and working as a team, and using basketball analogies to get the student excited and engaged in non-preferred tasks. All of this information can be used to your advantage when writing and implementing IEPs!

- **Work samples chosen by the student**: Was there a lesson the student really enjoyed, or a craft the student made that they are really proud of? Or maybe the student wants to show the team a lesson they really didn't enjoy or have fun with. Showcase that data at the meeting and allow the student to share why they chose to include different work samples.

- **Pictures of the student learning in the classroom**: All of the preceding is great information and data for the team to use in making data-driven decisions, but you know that pictures also speak a thousand words. You might even allow the student to take pictures of their favorite parts of the school, with their friends, or of their work.

- **Student progress and grade reports**: You might even have the student graph their IEP progress monitoring data or have the student self-monitor a goal or two. Students can then showcase their progress at the IEP meeting.

- **Any other items of the student's choosing.**

There is more prep for you as the teacher in this phase of conducting student-led IEPs, and my advice to you is to find what works best for you, your classroom, and your students. Find ways to integrate these advocacy activities into your daily schedule and work on different pieces of the student's portfolio throughout the school year, not just before an IEP meeting is scheduled.

And how a student participates in their IEP meeting will vary, especially before transition age. It might look like the student attending the first 10 minutes of the meeting to share their portfolio, a quick 5-minute prerecorded video of the child sharing their portfolio, the student attending during only a specific part of the discussion, or the student attending for the whole IEP meeting. In conversations with your student's parents and the IEP team, you will find what works best for that individual student.

One of the most fun ways to present a student portfolio at the IEP meeting is by creating a PowerPoint or Google Slides presentation. Students can aid in the creation of the slide deck and even present it at the beginning of their IEP meeting, or record themselves presenting the slide deck, and the prerecorded video can be shared at the meeting.

Amendment IEP Meeting

You may have worked with a student who mastered an IEP goal or goals quicker than expected, and you want to write a new IEP goal or goals for the child.

Other scenarios an amendment IEP meeting might be held include, but are not limited to:

- Addition or removal of services or supports.
- IEP team member requests change of services, supports, or placement.

You may hear the title "revision meeting" in your professional world, and it is important to know that a revision meeting is held to make updates to current IEP goals, while amendment meetings serve to make changes to the current IEP before the annual IEP meeting due date. In some states, these two meeting names are used interchangeably.

Amendment meetings may also occur without an official meeting. Outlined in Section 300.324,[11] the school and parent may agree to not convene a meeting to amend or modify the child's IEP, and if changes are made to a child's IEP, the public agency (school) must ensure that the child's IEP team is notified of the changes.

A revision or amendment IEP meeting does not take the place of an annual IEP meeting or change the due date of the child's upcoming annual IEP.

Reevaluation IEP Meeting

At a minimum, a child must be reevaluated for special education eligibility every three years. The purpose of the reevaluation is to see if the child's needs have changed, and also to see if the child still requires special education services to access the general education curriculum. This three-year reevaluation needs to be comprehensive, and typically includes the same evaluations that were completed during initial eligibility or the previous evaluation.

You may also hear this called the student's Triennial Review or Triennial Evaluation.

Discipline Review Meeting

This type of IEP meeting occurs when a student has been suspended or expelled from school, or received disciplinary action against them, like being sent home early due to a behavioral incident.

You also need to write a Manifestation Determination on the incident to determine:

- Was the behavior caused by, or have a direct and substantial relationship to, the child's disability?
- Was the behavior the direct result of the school's failure to implement the child's IEP?[12]

If the IEP team answers "yes" to either question, then it is determined that the child's behavior was a manifestation of their disability.

The purpose of this IEP meeting is to review the incident and any disciplinary action taken, discuss how to prevent the same type of incident from happening in the future, and create a plan for responding to similar incidents should they occur again. It may also be determined that a Functional Behavior Assessment (FBA) will need to be conducted to write a Behavior Intervention Plan (BIP) for the student, or that a new FBA/BIP will need to be done or the current FBA/BIP reevaluated.

Manifestation meetings must be held within 10 school days if the child has been suspended for 10 consecutive days, has been suspended for more than 10 days total in one school year for similar behaviors, or the school is considering expulsion.

Dismissal IEP Meeting

This type of meeting occurs when it is believed and backed up with data that a child can be dismissed from special education services. During a dismissal IEP meeting, parents should be encouraged to provide input regarding their child's progress.

The result of a dismissal IEP meeting does not automatically mean the child will be dismissed from special education services. It may be found and determined by the IEP team that the child will continue with the same program or changes to the child's IEP may be deemed more appropriate. Regardless of the outcome, it is important that parents have their voices heard throughout the process.

Any member of the IEP team can call for an IEP meeting at any time throughout the school year for any reason. The best course of action is to put the request in writing for school professionals or parents.

Amendments, or revisions, to the IEP can happen at any time during the calendar year, and as many times as needed throughout the year. Amendments can happen for a variety of reasons, including but not limited to mastery of goals, limited progress made on goals, or changes to services or supports.

Remember that amendment meetings do not take the place of the annual IEP meeting, or extend the dates of the annual IEP. For example, if a child's annual IEP meeting is December 1 and the team had three amendment IEP meetings, with the last being on September 15, the team will still meet to review the IEP at the annual IEP meeting on or before December 1 of the following year.

An IEP versus a 504 Plan

IEPs are protected under the Individuals with Disabilities Act and are for students who are found eligible for special education services. However, some students may receive supports under a 504 plan. These plans are covered under Section 504 of the Rehabilitation Act of 1973, which is a federal civil rights law enacted to stop discrimination against people with disabilities.

Remember, to be eligible for an IEP under IDEA, the child must meet two criteria:

- The child must have a disability that adversely affects their educational performance.
- As a result of the disability, the child needs special education services to make progress in school and learn the general education curriculum.

To be eligible for a 504 plan, the student must be determined to:

- Have a physical or mental impairment that substantially limits one or more major life activities.
- Have a record of such an impairment.
- Be regarded as having such an impairment.

When this determination is made, the student must also meet the following two requirements:

- Have any disability.
- The disability must interfere with the child's ability to learn in the general education classroom.

When it comes to IEPs, the IDEA law is super-specific. Section 504 has a broader definition of a disability than IDEA does. Section 504 of the Rehabilitation Act says, "a disability must substantially limit one or more major life activities." This can include caring for one's self, walking, seeing, hearing, speaking, breathing, learning, working, and so on. This is why a child who doesn't qualify for an IEP might still be able to get a 504 plan.

Decisions about which educational and related services are appropriate for a student under Section 504 must be made by a team of individuals who are knowledgeable about the student, the evaluation data, and placement options. Table 1.2 outlines more of the differences between IEPs and 504 plans.

IEPs are written documents that set annual learning goals for a student and include many different sections. A 504 plan varies widely, and generally only includes accommodations, supports, and services. These regulations vary by state. It's also important to note that a 504 plan does not need to be written down, unlike an IEP.

Table 1.2 Some Differences between an IEP and a 504 Plan

IEP	504 Plan
From IDEA; a written document that sets annual learning goals and includes many sections.	From Section 504 of the Rehabilitation Act of 1973; generally only includes accommodations, supports, and/or services.
To qualify, a child (1) must be formally diagnosed with having a disability that is one of the 13 categories outlined in the federal law, and (2) as a result of the disability, the child needs special education services to make progress in school and learn the general education curriculum.	To qualify, a child (1) can have any disability, and (2) the disability must interfere with the child's ability to learn in the general education classroom.
Documentation includes a written document that sets annual learning goals and includes many sections.	Documentation includes only accommodations, supports, and/or services, and these vary by state.
A parent or guardian must provide consent, and they must be notified in writing of any proposed changes.	A parent or guardian must provide consent. Proposed changes do not need to be in writing.
Service plan is reviewed annually.	Service plan is reviewed annually.
No cost, as the funds come from IDEA.	No cost. There is no additional state funding for 504 plans. IDEA funds may not be used on 504 plan services.

When it comes to consent of and for a 504 plan, the child's parent or caregiver must provide consent, and any time a change is proposed the family must be notified. A key difference here is that this notification does not have to be in writing, as with an IEP, although many schools do provide a written proposal for changes.

Each child will have a 504 team, but the regulations on this team are much looser than the requirements of who is on a child's IEP team. Most times, a child's 504 team includes the parent or caregiver, the child's teachers, and an administrator.

Like an IEP, 504 plans are typically reviewed annually, as with IEPs, but the regulations may vary by state.

Just like IEPs, 504 plans are provided to students at no cost. And unlike IEPs where states receive additional funding for students with disabilities, the states do not receive funding for 504 plans and any IDEA funds provided to a state may not be used to provide 504 plan services.

Summary

Laws and policies that are in place today were set to protect individuals with disabilities, and provide them with services and supports that will carry them through their lifetime. In a perfect world, IEP teams would not need to fight so hard for rights that disabled individuals deserve, but with the knowledge you have learned so far you are well on your way to becoming a very strong advocate for your students and their families. Your advocacy will help shape the future, and that's pretty stinkin' cool!

Notes

1. https://www.govinfo.gov/content/pkg/STATUTE-77/pdf/STATUTE-77-Pg282.pdf
2. https://sites.ed.gov/idea/IDEA-History
3. https://sites.ed.gov/idea/IDEA-History

4. *Board of Education of the Hendrick Hudson Central School District v. Amy Rowley*, 458 U.S. 176 (1982), https://supreme.justia.com/cases/federal/us/458/176/

5. https://case-law.vlex.com/vid/irving-independent-school-district-893158613

6. https://nces.ed.gov/programs/coe/indicator/cgg/students-with-disabilities

7. https://sites.ed.gov/idea/files/Alignment_with_NCLB_2-2-07.pdf

8. https://sites.ed.gov/idea/IDEA-History

9. https://health.wusf.usf.edu/health-news-florida/2022-12-06/many-kids-are-struggling-is-special-education-the-answer

10. Section 300.301.

11. law.cornell.edu/cfr/text/34/300.324

12. https://www.pacer.org/parent/php/PHP-c285.pdf

Chapter 2
Data Collection

Objective 1	Learner will glean multiple progress monitoring tools and develop a system that works in their classroom.
Objective 2	Learner will establish a system for analyzing data.
Objective 3	Learner will use data to make decisions at the IEP table and determine next steps for IEP goal skills.

If the word *IEP* doesn't immediately overwhelm a teacher's soul, then *data* might very well do the job. When it comes to data collection, there are a lot of variables and moving parts. Just like IEP writing is a team effort, data collection should be too. Meaningful data collection starts with writing meaningful IEP goals that are clearly defined and specific. If you look at an IEP goal and have no idea what skill you are monitoring, it's time to rewrite the goal. And just as the *Present Levels* (the student's current level of academic and functional performance that is described more in Chapter 3) guide you to what IEP goals to write, your IEP goals will guide you to what data to collect and how to showcase mastery. But before you can dive into the how, you have to know the what . . . and the where, when, who, and why.

The Five Ws of Data Collection

Who should be collecting data?	Any adult or professional who works with a child who has an IEP.
Where should data be collected?	Across all settings that the child is in throughout the school day.
When should data be collected?	Data should be collected every day, even if it is only informal observation data.
What should data be collected on?	Data should be collected on IEP goals and objectives, as well as any baseline data needed to make additional suggestions or changes to the child's IEP.
Why do you collect data?	As a special educator, it's your job—but also, you need to have enough data to make data-driven decisions at the IEP table. Data is evidence of needing supports, or not needing supports, and it is the simplest way to measure progress. Without data, any suggestions are merely opinions.

But the big question is how? You may have everyone on board to take data, but how do you collect the data in an efficient manner? Because to be effective, progress monitoring needs to be quick and easy to administer so that you can easily analyze the data to determine if the student is responding effectively to the instruction, interventions, supports, and services. In addition, for progress monitoring, you need to determine how often data will be taken officially and how often progress will be reported. When it comes to progress reporting, schools typically write "with grade reporting" into the IEP. The team determines how often to report progress in relation to the school's standard, and this should be determined based on the intensity of the instruction and interventions. It's important to remember, too, that it's not the quantity or the quality of the data you take, but rather how you are using this information to make decisions about effective instruction and interventions. When you change and update your instructional methods and interventions based on the data, you should expect to see student learning increase.

Keep in mind that there is no one right or wrong way to progress monitor IEP goals and objectives. What matters most is how you use the data to make decisions.

There are many types of tools and assessments that you can use for progress monitoring:

- **Screening assessments** are used to identify students who are on target and students who need different, more intense levels of supports. Students who are identified on the screening assessments as needing more assistance should be given a diagnostic assessment.
- **Diagnostic assessments** give you more in-depth knowledge regarding a student's strengths and impairments, and you will most often use diagnostics to determine appropriate interventions and supports.
- **Progress monitoring tools** are ongoing and provide the IEP team with continuous feedback on how the student is performing and whether you need to modify instruction more or less, or try different interventions. Progress monitoring tools can use formal and informal assessment types, and should be utilized by all members of the IEP team.

Data Collection Methods

When it comes to progress monitoring tools, there are a lot of options to choose from, and it can be difficult to keep your blinders on. Sticky notes, data sheets, digital forms, apps . . . all claiming to be the best way to collect data. As an educator, being flexible is your biggest ally when it comes to progress monitoring. What works for one student may not work for another. What works one year may not work the next. What works for progress monitoring one skill may not work for another skill. My biggest suggestion is to soak in all the methods and information like a sponge, and then mold what you've learned into a data collection method that works just for you and your students. To provide you with an ample starting point, I want to teach you about the two most popular methods—sticky note data collection and digital data collection using digital forms.

Sticky Note Data Collection

Supplies: The only supplies you need for this method are sticky notes, a writing utensil, and your binder rings (see the appendix). There is no specific size, shape, color, or brand of sticky notes that works better, and the same goes for your writing utensils. I prefer to stock up on sticky notes at the beginning of the school year when all the school supplies are on sale.

How: First and foremost, the anatomy of your sticky note is of vital importance. You want to make sure that where you're putting the key information follows a format that you can read and analyze, and that the team can also implement, read, and analyze it. See Figure 2.1.

- In the top-left corner, put the name of the activity. You can use abbreviations, just make sure it's an abbreviation that you will remember when it comes time to inputting and analyzing the data.
- In the top-right corner, write the date and put a box around it. Why a box? This is so you don't get the date mixed up with any of your data points. Some month and date variations can look like data points, for example January 10 can be written 1/10. If you are collecting data on an activity with 10 questions or trials, the date may very well get mixed in with your data. To prevent this mistake, putting a box around the date reminds you that 1/10 is the date the data was collected.

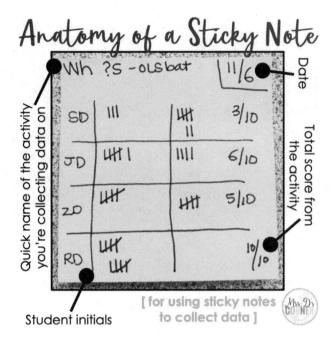

Figure 2.1 Here Is How to Set Up Your Sticky Notes to Effectively Collect Data Using the Sticky Data Method.

- In the middle of the sticky note is where you collect your data points, and you want to keep it simple. Use tally marks or + and − to show correct and incorrect responses. If you are collecting data on multiple students at the same time, or collecting data on multiple trials in one sitting, you can divide this part of your sticky note into sections. With tally marks, I like to divide the middle into two sections: one side for correct responses and the other for incorrect responses. If I am using + and −, I write the student responses in sequential order. See Figure 2.2.
- On the bottom left side, you put the student initials. If you're working with multiple students, you can put all of their initials and align the data points with the correct student.
- On the bottom right side, after you've collected the data, you write the final data point. If the student was provided 10 questions and they got 6 correct and 4 incorrect, you would write 6/10.

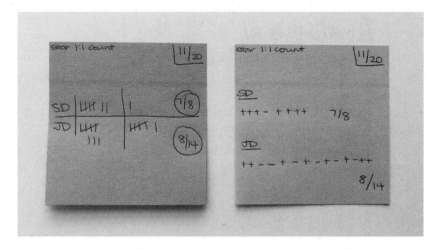

Figure 2.2 You Can Collect Data Using the Sticky Data Method and Use the +/- or Tally Marks, and the Result Will Be the Same Based on the Child's Responses During the Trial.

Coming up with your own system for codes and shortcuts helps with data collection too! For example, writing "VP" next to a child's data point or on the sticky note might tell you that Verbal Prompts were provided during the trial, or "RA" means that read aloud was provided. As long as the team is using the same codes and shortcuts when progress monitoring, it can be a helpful tool in making a data-driven decision at the IEP table.

Once you've taken data using the sticky note, transfer this data into something or somewhere that won't be lost or misplaced. I prefer to use the Progress Monitoring Binder Rings (see the appendix) because it allows me to have all data points for all IEP goals for one specific student in one place. Throughout the week, I make a pile of data sticky notes in one designated place. At the end of the week, either I or a para will transfer the data points to respective student binder rings. Then, when it comes time to write progress reports, the only thing you'll need to grab is each student's binder rings and you're ready to get writing (see Figure 2.3). To learn more about data rings, visit www.mrsdscorner.com/progressmonitoring madequickeasy.

You can also transform this method into a larger data sheet for yourself, putting all of a student's IEP goals and objectives on one sheet of paper. Again, it's all in one place and easy to grab to input and output data.

Pros of This Method	Cons of This Method
Simple and effective.	May not provide enough space to collect data.
Can take the data anywhere at any time.	Might lose a sticky note or two.
Can be taught to other team members very quickly.	You need to input this data manually into a graph to analyze it.
All data points are in one place.	

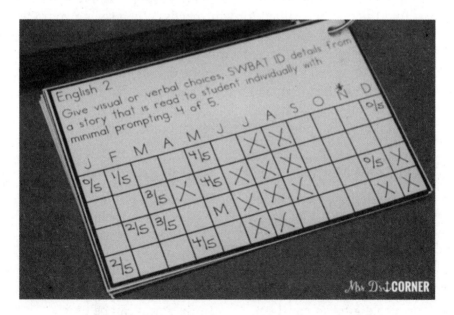

Figure 2.3 Data Rings Organize Student Information into One Place.

Digital Data Collection

Supplies: For digital data collection, you need some type of technology, like a tablet, phone, or computer, and a Google account to use Google Forms. Not necessary, but you can also integrate QR codes with this method, so access to a QR code generator may be helpful.

How: With digital data collection, it is best to set everything up at the beginning of the school year. This can be labor intensive, but it is worth it in the long run. Your first step is creating your classroom folder, and then creating a folder for each student on your caseload. Inside each folder is where you create Google Forms for the IEP goals you will be monitoring digitally. You can purchase my digital forms at Mrs. D's Corner on www.teacherspayteachers .com. Each IEP goal or objective will get its own form, and what each form looks like will be different based on the data you need to collect to show mastery of the skill.

Once you've created all the needed folders and forms, you can take the link to each form and generate a QR code for it. There are free QR code generators online, so a simple Google search will help you find the one best suited for your needs. When saving your QR code images, make sure to save each image as the student's name and what the goal is to prevent a mix-up. You can then take all of a student's QR codes, paste them into one document, label each QR code, print the document and a cover sheet, and put this on a clipboard. This clipboard can then be accessed by any team member to take data on the student's goals across different settings.

Pros of This Method	Cons of This Method
All team members have access to the same forms at all times.	Technology can break and needs to be recharged frequently. Have a backup plan!
Can be taught to other team members very quickly.	
All data points are in one place.	No compatibility with the technology you own or use.
Can easily graph data points using a digital spreadsheet.	Initial setup can be time consuming.

Always make sure the digital tool you are using prioritizes the security of your student's data. Confidentiality of student information must be kept at the forefront.

With any progress monitoring tool, you want to make sure that you are consistent. Consistent progress monitoring helps you identify patterns and trends and ultimately helps you analyze the data. If your data is inconsistent, it will be very difficult to graph it and compare your intervention data to your baseline data.

Paraprofessionals Helping with Data Collection

When it comes to data collection, it's all hands on deck. Your paraprofessionals can and should be helping you progress monitor on all student IEP goals, especially if they are working with that child. But it's not as simple as asking them to collect data. This is not a free-for-all; you must have a game plan.

The first part of the plan is you deciding how you will collect data on all student IEP goals and which progress monitoring tools you will use. The next step is making sure the tool is set up and ready to be used, so you can then model. You will model how to use it, when to use it, what to use it on, and so forth. In addition to modeling, your paraprofessionals need to be provided with explicit training, which can be done in congruence with modeling. This step may take the longest, but the success of your para taking data relies heavily on their understanding of the progress monitoring tools you've selected. After that, it's time for your para to start taking data. It's important for you to provide feedback (and praise!) and allow an open dialogue to occur so that constructive feedback can occur from both parties—you and your para. Your para serves as your eyes and ears, and they may notice something you have not yet noticed. Training and modeling is important, but collaboration and communication are key!

Once your para is taking data and your system is flowing, it becomes easier to not only collect more data, but also to update your instructional methods and interventions based on the data, which should lead you to an increase in student learning.

Students Helping with Their Data Collection

Students are valuable resources when it comes to progress monitoring too, even more so than the data you or I might collect when it comes to certain IEP goals. How a student thinks or feels about an activity, a support, or even the IEP goal itself can make or break that student's progress. Your students are more than capable of helping with data collection! Here are a few ideas along with guiding questions to help get you started:

- Complete a survey about how the student thinks they did, or how well the student thinks the lesson went. *How did it go? What would you change or do differently?*
- Emotional regulation scale before, during, and after an activity. *How did you feel?*
- Share how useful a support or service was during a lesson. *Was your accommodation of X helpful? Tell why or why not.*
- Student-corrected assignments. *What percent did you get correct? How can you do better next time?*
- Student-graded assignments using a rubric. *What grade do you think you achieved and why? What supports helped, or what help did you need?*
- Allow the student to collect and keep track of work samples. *What are you proud of and why?*
- Have students create their own learning goals and keep track of progress. *What goal would you like to set, and how can you get there?*

You can learn more about student self-advocacy and how to get students involved in their IEP process in Chapter 1.

How you collect data is not as important as ensuring that you do.

Common Data Collection Questions and Answers

Can you give students different work samples on the same goal or does it all need to be exactly the same?

When you are writing IEP goals, remember that you shouldn't be using one standard measurement, or criteria, for skill mastery. The IEP goal trials also shouldn't be one specific amount of problems or questions per progress monitoring session. Best practice tells us to use multiple sources of data to make decisions, and to get multiple sources of data you will need to use different probes, assessments, and resources to get the data.

All of this to say, you want the student to demonstrate skill mastery and generalization of the skill proves mastery. You don't want to give the student the same exact worksheet, set of flash cards, book to read, or activity to complete. Successful completion of one worksheet shows that the student can complete that specific worksheet, and does not demonstrate mastery of the skill.

Does each trial need to be identical, and does a trial need to happen at the same time each day?

Piggybacking off of the last question, your trials should not be identical every single time because you want the child to generalize the skill, that is, use the skill under different conditions. And the size of your trial does not need to be the same each time either. For example, let's pretend this is your student's IEP goal:

Given 20 flash cards of Dolch Primer sight words, the student will be able to identify and fluently read each sight word with 65% accuracy in four of five trials.

Your student is waiting for the speech pathologist to arrive, and other students are headed to specials. This transition gives you a quick minute or two to assess the student on the given IEP goal. You grab a sticky note to keep data on how many words the student gets correct, but you did not have time to go through 20 flash cards. You only got through 13. No big, this still counts as a trial. Out of the 13 sight words, the student was able to identify and fluently read 11 sight words. That's 11/13. You can then turn the 11/13 into a fraction, which then can be turned into a percent. Once you have the percentage, which would be 85% for this trial, you will look to see if that meets the mastery criteria of the goal. The mastery criteria is 65%, so with 11/13 correct responses, the student would have met the mastery criteria for that trial.

How do you schedule data collection into your school day?

Every teacher is going to use progress monitoring tools to fit their own specific classroom and student needs. But that's not to say you can't schedule mass data collection at a specific time each week. For example, every Wednesday afternoon students work in IEP bins or out of their green folders, both of which would have specific, individualized activities that align with student IEP goals. Here are three different ways I've built mass data collection into my classrooms:

1. When I taught 5th-grade math resource, my students each had a yellow folder, and on Friday morning I would work with individual students or small groups on specific skills, while the other students worked out of their yellow folders. Friday afternoons we would have Fun Friday, where students would rotate through centers and play board games, listen to audiobooks or music, have tablet time, and so on. While students were engaging in Fun Friday, I would go through yellow folders to collect data and work samples. Monday mornings, based on Friday's data, I would put more activities inside of yellow folders and adjust interventions and supports as needed.

2. When I taught 1st- through 4th-grade life skills, my classroom utilized color-coded IEP work bins. Each student had their own bin, and inside that bin were different activities that aligned with their IEP goals. Each afternoon, there was designated time in our schedule to work out of our IEP bins. Activities inside the bins

would be rotated on a weekly and biweekly basis, depending on the student and what the data was telling me. This allowed us to work on multiple skills at the same time, both modified grade-level skills and prerequisite skills. For example, if a student's peers were learning about telling time on an analog clock to the minute, that student might be working on the parts of a clock, including number recognition, during our math block and then additional math skills during IEP bin time based on IEP goals.

3. When I taught Extended School Year for a mild-moderate first-grade class, each of my students had a folder that traveled with them during center time. Center time was a two-hour timeframe in the morning before lunch, and centers were set up in a way that facilitated a work-play-work-play mind set. Each center lasted no more than 20 minutes, and we had six centers in total, which means there were three academic centers and three play centers. Academic centers were run by me and two paraprofessionals. Play centers included things like puzzles, music, books, and fine-motor and sensory toys. Inside of each student's folder were data sheets for a specific IEP goals they were to be working on during ESY, and every week, my paras and I would swap centers so we could collaboratively collect data on all skills. This format kept students engaged during the majority of our morning, kept adults engaged by switching centers up each week, and ultimately, helped us collect a lot of data for the regular school year teacher and build skills during the summer for those students.

One important point to note about any mass scheduled method is that you should also be taking additional data throughout the day, and across settings. This set time in your schedule should not be the one and only time that you are progress monitoring on IEP goals. Rather, it should be scheduled time for you to work on specific skills with your students and assess any changes to interventions and supports.

Should you set deadlines for collecting data before the IEP meeting?

Ideally, yes. If a student's IEP meeting is coming up on April 4 and it is April 3, your data collection should be completed, analyzed, and graphed—ready to share at the IEP meeting to support your IEP table proposals. Looking at the IEP Writing Timeline in Figure 1.1 from Chapter 1, best practice shows that all of your data collection should be done before you begin writing the child's Present Levels. Why? You need that data to write the Present Levels, including baseline data. If you are sending home the proposed draft IEP prior to the IEP meeting, all of your data needs to be in the Present Levels ready to back up your proposed IEP goals. You have flexibility, though, in setting a deadline for your IEP teams to have all of their data in to you. I suggest setting one timeframe—for example, the data is due three weeks before the IEP meeting—and sticking to it for each student.

How much data should you collect to show accuracy?

Your school will often dictate how many data points you need to collect each week or each marking period, and just like a lot of other IEP stuff, there isn't one set number of data points that will show you mastery of a skill. This is where the importance of analyzing the data points lies.

Analyzing Data

Have you ever tried the experiment with your students where you have an object in a box? You know what it is, but your students do not. They are allowed to reach into the box to touch the object, but they are not allowed to look in the box. Inside the box is dark, they don't know if the object is slimy or smooth, big or small, alive or inanimate, or if it makes noise. They trust you, but they put their hand unwillingly inside the box to make a hypothesis about what they think the object is.

Not analyzing your data is similar. Parents trust you because you are the professional, but you aren't really sure what's going on because you can't see inside the box (you haven't analyzed the data). Analyzing data is just as important as taking data because your data is useless if you don't use it.

There isn't a set rule for how many data points a team needs to make a decision, but you do need enough data to be able to notice trends and patterns. And when you are analyzing data, you need to make sure the baseline data is included in your analysis. You want to think "where did the student start?" and "what data points will show progress or regression of this skill?" When you start thinking about the beginning and the end result the team is aiming for, you can then hypothesize about how many data points may be needed over what period of time to show growth or regression while also thinking about what interventions and supports the child will need to get there. This conversation is a part of the IEP meeting and should be discussed when the team is determining IEP goal criteria and progress reporting.

As you are collecting data, it is equally as important to organize your data as it is to analyze it. How you choose to organize your data is up to you, but it is important to have an established system and keep it. How you are taking your data may also lead you to use one method over another. The next sections describe a couple of organization systems that may work for you.

Using File Folders

Probably the most widely used method of organization is keeping all data points and work samples in file folders. One file folder can be used for one specific IEP goal, one subject, or for all student data and information. You can also color code the file folders for ease (green is for science, blue is for math, yellow is for ELA, and so on).

- **File Folders in Hanging Folders**—Keeping file folders in hanging folders is a great option for teachers who have less storage, but have access to a filing cabinet. You can house multiple file folders within one hanging folder too!
- **File Folders in Project Cases**—Project cases are a great option for storing student work samples and data in one closed case inside of your filing drawer or a cabinet. You can easily remove the project case to take it to meetings or to share data with the team at any time and not have to worry about items falling out of a larger folder. This option takes up more space, but multiple items can be stored inside.

- **Student IEP Binders or Notebooks**—IEP binders or notebooks are a great option for keeping all of a student's information in one place, including a copy of the IEP, notes from home, work samples, and progress notes. Use plastic binder sleeves to store information by week or marking period, or simply hole-punch any document to add it to the binder. Binders and notebooks can be color coded as well. This is my preferred method.
- **Digital Organization**—Works great for those using digital data collection! Create a digital folder where all of a student's information is kept, including digital data forms. Student work samples can be uploaded into the digital folder by taking a picture of the work sample or scanning it using the school's copier.

Regardless of which organization system you choose to implement, there are two key components you must keep in mind:

- All of your data points should be dated and put in numerical order to establish a timeline.
- Keep multiple student work samples that align with a few of your data points.

It's not necessary to keep all student work samples, but it will be necessary to show work related to the skill during your data analysis. Once you have your data organization system in place and your data is organized, it's time to graph your data.

Graphing the Data

Graphing your data helps paint a picture and provides a visual representation of the data that can easily be interpreted by the student's IEP team. Graphs also help you notice trends and more easily pinpoint when interventions are working or not working. There are three types of graphs that work best for this type of data analysis:

- **Line graphs** are helpful to compare a lot of data points at once to show trends over a period of time. On a line graph, the data points generally have a connection to one another.

- **Bar graphs** help when grouping data points together, and they are very helpful in showing larger trends in data points over time.
- **Scatter plot graphs** are helpful in showing the relationship between two variables that complement one another. You can project a student's progress and then graph the child's data points around the projection to see if the child is making adequate progress.

But how do you choose which graph to use? This will depend on the skill you want to graph. When determining which graph to use, you want to think "what type of graph will best showcase this student's data?" or "which graph will be the best option for telling the data's story?"

Let's take a look at these two examples:

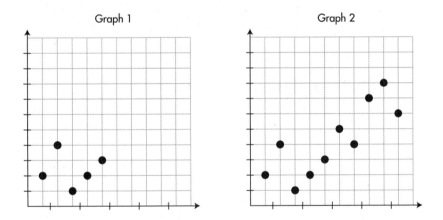

Which set of data points paints a better picture of the child's progress? In Graph 1, you see a spike in progress, a sharp decline, and then steady progress. In Graph 2, you see the same beginning, but with more data points you're also able to notice a trend that when the student has an increase in progress, shortly after there is a slight decrease in progress. The student then continues advancing to make additional progress. This is a trend and can help you make decisions at the IEP table.

If your data points stopped after the fifth data point in Graph 1, you would not have been able to glean more information about the child's progress toward mastery of this skill. If you find yourself analyzing data points similar to Graph 1, your proposal to the team may be that data is inconclusive at this time or more data is needed to notice trends in progress. All data helps you make decisions at the IEP table.

Data should be analyzed more than once a school year. It's important to set time aside to organize and graph your data points at least once a month, or every couple of weeks. While that sounds like a huge undertaking, and it may be, you will thank yourself later when it comes time to write progress reports or the student's IEP. You can have other team members, including paraprofessionals, help you with data graphing and analysis. Remember, don't IEP alone!

Let's take a look at another example:

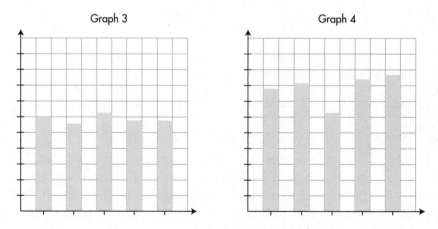

In looking at Graph 3, what can you hypothesize about the child's progress? According to the bar graph, the student is staying steady around the same knowledge point but is not making any progress or regressing. This data is telling us it might be time to

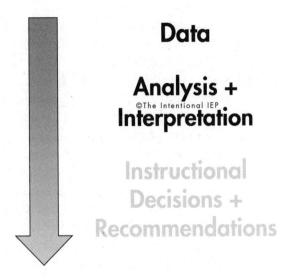

Figure 2.4 Once You've Analyzed and Interpreted the Data, You Use the Data to Make Instructional Decisions and Recommendations.

change interventions and supports. What about Graph 4? You can see the student is making steady progress, with one outlier of data in week 3. When the team dives in further, it might be discovered that the child had a substitute teacher that week, which skewed the data a little. But you wouldn't know that information unless you analyzed all of the data and information at hand.

Data is more than points on a graph. If you notice a trend or outlier data point, it's the team's job to not only look deeper into what a possible cause may have been, but also determine and investigate the use of interventions and supports. Because graphing is just the tip of the iceberg when it comes to data analysis. You have to then use the data to make decisions and recommendations, as illustrated in Figure 2.4.

Making Decisions with Data

All of your hard work and dedication has circled back around to the student's IEP meeting and it's time to turn the data into action. Your analysis and graphing is complete, and you need to share your findings with the team. To start, remind the team of the student's IEP goals and objectives, or the reason why the data was collected. You can then discuss any baseline data that was taken and dive right into the graphs you made to make comparisons. It is best practice to go over one set of IEP goal data at a time. Share your analysis findings and any student work samples, and allow the team to provide feedback and insight on their understanding of the data. This is the team's time to ask questions, decide which interventions worked or did not work, and ultimately, determine what skills need to be worked on next.

Here's an example of how this IEP table conversation may look:

Student IEP Goal	Given a modified grade level text, Oliver will verbally make inferences and use text evidence to support his understanding of the text when the text is read to him with 60% accuracy in three of four trials.
Baseline Data	Oliver is a 2nd-grade student reading at the beginning reader stage. He can read a DRA 2 kindergarten passage fluently with 91% accuracy. Baseline: He is able to perform this skill with 24% accuracy without supports and 39% accuracy with supports.
Graphs + Comparisons	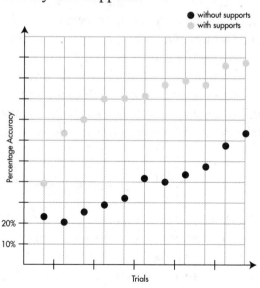

| Analysis Findings | Interventions and supports provided to Oliver through this annual IEP have been successful, and Oliver has mastered this IEP goal. The team decides to keep all current supports in place. |
| Suggestions | Recommended IEP goal of making connections in a given text to personal experiences or other texts. |

Here are some questions to think about and pose to the team when using data to make decisions:

- How often was data collected on this skill, and was enough data collected to showcase trends and adjust interventions and supports?
- How often was data analyzed over the last year and was it sufficient in recognizing a need for adjusted interventions or supports?
- What do the trends in the data tell you about the student's mastery or needs?
- Are the current interventions helping or holding the student back?
- Has the student demonstrated an increased mastery of the skill or accomplished the goal? Why or why not?
- Is the data consistent with the team's projections of student progress over the last year?
- Are there any gaps in the data? If yes, why?
- What curriculum or materials are needed to address the student's needs in the upcoming annual IEP?

Always remember the reason you are taking and analyzing data: to evaluate progress and adjust interventions as needed. Know that your data analysis may not lead you to an exact solution or intervention, so it is important to continue with data collection to ensure the intervention or support chosen is appropriate for the student. Progress monitoring never stops, and you may find yourself at an amendment or revision IEP meeting throughout the year to make changes to a student's IEP based on the data (*this is why it's important to analyze data frequently*). It's important to remember, too, that it's okay to change your data collection method or progress monitoring tools after you've analyzed the data. Just like writing the actual IEP, nothing is set in stone, and it can be changed or updated at any time.

Reverse Planning IEP Goals with Data

You've almost reached the finish line to close out your data collection circle. You have analyzed the student's annual IEP data, followed the IEP writing timeline, received feedback from team members via input forms, written the Present Levels, and you are ready to propose IEP goals based on all of the data. The easiest way to write IEP goals based on data is to write them backward. Not phonetically or structurally, but in a reverse planning way. There are four steps to reverse planning for IEP goal writing; each is covered next.

Step 1: Look at the Data

No surprise here, your data is the first step even when reverse planning. You need to know what skills the student does possess, how the student is performing alongside same-aged peers, what strengths the student has, and what supports and services have been helpful. You need to have a general understanding of how much progress the student can realistically achieve in one academic year.

Step 2: Look at the Grade-Level Standards

What skills are the student's grade-level, neurotypical peers expected to learn? Many states now require IEPs, and more specifically IEP goals, to be standards-aligned, which you learn more about in Chapter 3. It's important to know what a student's peers are learning, so you know what supports and services the student will need to achieve mastery of the IEP goal you will be proposing to the team. This information also gives you a great starting point for determining any necessary prerequisite skills.

Step 3: Look at the Standard's Prerequisite Skills

What foundational skills must this student learn to be able to learn higher level skills? And what foundational skills must this student learn to function independently now and later in life? For example, a student cannot perform addition and subtraction if they have not yet mastered 1:1 correspondence. A student cannot perform algebraic operations if they have not yet mastered foundational computation skills.

Some prerequisite skills are easier to determine than others, and the others may take a little more digging to figure out what foundational skills are needed to achieve a grade level standard. If your school does not provide you with any scaffolding or vertical alignment documents to help you determine prerequisites, start by using your state's content standards. Most state standards from grade to grade are connected and build on one another, making them a great free resource to utilize when determining prerequisite skills.

Step 4: Determine Where Your Student Needs to Go

Based on the data, what skills are of highest priority for this annual IEP, and what foundational skills is the student lacking that are necessary for independence, in comparison to the student's same-aged peers? In answering this key question, you will use your knowledge from Steps 1–3 to determine which skill an IEP goal should be written for.

Just as important as the skill an IEP goal is written for is the baseline data you collect on the skill. Baseline data serves as your benchmark, or starting data point, and is collected to make comparisons after interventions and supports are implemented. Baseline data should be collected on the skill in question and should be collected with and without supports. You want your data to reflect a true baseline, so when supports are added or changed, you can analyze the data to adjust.

There is no definitive number for how many IEP goals can be written into a student's IEP. While a team cannot appropriately work toward mastery of, for example, 30 new academic skills in one school year, it may be found through data analysis that the student is lacking many important foundational skills. Determining how many IEP goals to write for one child in an academic year is a team decision, and skill priorities should always be at the forefront of the conversation, alongside what is realistic for that child to master in one academic year.

Writing IEP Goals with Data Collection in Mind

It is time to close out your data collection ring to begin the process again, and the very last step to close your data collection circle is to write the IEP goal criteria. The goal criteria specifies how the student will demonstrate mastery of the skill. Here are the different types of goal criteria:

- Accuracy.
- Frequency.
- Duration.
- Rate.
- Distance.
- Intensity.
- Latency.

When writing an IEP goal, some skills lend themselves better to one type of criteria over another, and just like reverse IEP goal planning, choosing the criteria is often best determined by working backward. When determining a goal's criteria, you want to answer these questions:

- What is the end result the team wants the student to achieve?
- What data does the team need to collect to showcase the student's learning in relation to achieving this goal? What story does the data need to tell?
- Which criteria will best allow the team to collect this data?

If you are writing an IEP goal for cutting along a line, you wouldn't use rate, intensity, or latency to accurately measure progress. And if you are writing an IEP goal for playing cooperatively in games with friends and peers, you probably won't use accuracy or distance to measure progress of that skill. See how some skills lend themselves better to one criteria type over another?

But choosing a goal's criteria is more than answering those questions. You also need to think about the data in the student's Present Levels and the area of the skill being assessed. The Present Levels helped you determine what skills to write IEP goals for, and you have the baseline data for these skills too!

So if a child's baseline data on a skill says they can perform a specific mathematics task with 12% accuracy, and overall can achieve an average of 40% increase of a math skill's mastery in an annual year based on data, you can infer that a realistic accuracy percentage would not be 90% accuracy for this child. Yes, you have high expectations for your students, but you also need to be realistic about what can be achieved in an annual year based on the data. Clarity is key and should be at the forefront of your mind as you set mastery criteria for each IEP goal and objective. Keep it clear and ensure that the criteria you choose really does encapsulate the end mastery goal for the student.

Summary

Collecting data is one of the most important jobs you have as a special education teacher and caseload manager. Data is used to measure progress on goals and help you write IEPs, and it tells you when and what interventions are and are not working throughout the school year. But data collection does not have to be cumbersome or overwhelming when you take the knowledge you've just learned and apply it to creating a system that works for you and your students. Stay flexible, don't do it all yourself, and follow where the data leads you!

Chapter 3
Writing the IEP

Objective 1	Learner will gather information about the sections of an IEP.
Objective 2	Learner will be able to write a strong Present Levels of Academic and Functional Performance section of the IEP.
Objective 3	Learner will write S.M.A.R.T. IEP goals and objectives and learn the difference between objectives and benchmarks.
Objective 4	Learner will determine the most appropriate supports and services for a student.
Objective 5	Learner will determine a child's Least Restrictive Environment (LRE).

IEPs give students legal protection and make it possible for parents and teachers to work together to provide students with disabilities an education. This means that IEPs are important! Knowledge is power, and when the IEP team is working together and on the same page, the student benefits with an individualized roadmap to success.

The federal IDEA law and your state's policies dictate student and family rights as well as everything else that goes into an IEP.

When the team sits down to write the IEP, there are key parts that every IEP must include according to the IDEA in Section 300.320:

- "A statement of the child's present levels of academic achievement and functional performance, including how the child's disability affects his or her involvement and progress in the general education curriculum.
- Measurable annual goals, including academic and functional goals.
- A description of how the child's progress toward meeting the annual goals will be measured, and when periodic progress reports will be provided.
- A statement of the special education and related services and supplementary aids and services to be provided to the child, or on behalf of the child.
- A statement of the program modifications or supports for school personnel that will be provided to enable the child to advance appropriately toward attaining the annual goals; to be involved in and make progress in the general education curriculum and to participate in extracurricular and other nonacademic activities; and to be educated and participate with other children with disabilities and nondisabled children.
- An explanation of the extent, if any, to which the child will not participate with nondisabled children in the regular class and in extracurricular and nonacademic activities.
- A statement of any individual accommodations that are necessary to measure the academic achievement and functional performance of the child on State and district-wide assessments.
- If the IEP team determines that the child must take an alternate assessment instead of a particular regular State or district-wide assessment of student achievement, the IEP must include a statement of why the child cannot participate in the regular assessment and why the particular alternate assessment selected is appropriate for the child.
- The projected date for the beginning of the services and modifications, and the anticipated frequency, location, and duration of those services and modifications."

As an IEP team, you also need to consider special factors, including any behaviors that may impede learning as well as special factors for your students who have limited English proficiency, are blind or visually impaired, and who are deaf or hard of hearing. And transition age kicks in at age 16, or sooner in your state. This means that as an IEP team, you need to consider the student's strengths; the student's academic, developmental, and functional needs; any concerns the team has; and any evaluation results and data.

Some states do require IEP teams to send a proposed IEP draft prior to the IEP meeting. It will be beneficial for you to learn your school's policy on draft IEPs as well as your state's regulations.

All of this is to say there are multiple parts, or sections, to an IEP. And while there are thousands of different IEP formats, the guts of what goes into an IEP are all the same. In this chapter, you learn about the key components of an IEP and what information should be included in each of these sections.

Student-Centered IEP Writing

When you begin writing an IEP, you are often taking baseline data, administering complex assessments, and getting anecdotal feedback and reports from adults and professionals who know the student best. This information helps guide what your students still need to know, and what you can focus the annual goals and benchmarks on. This information allows you to determine what additional supports students need, and what setting the student needs to make the most progress due to the deficits compiled through the data.

(continued)

(continued)

What you do not want to do with this information is to transcribe it as it is directly into a child's IEP. An IEP was never designed to be a deficit-focused document. It is important to remember the audience of an IEP, especially in the meeting. The individuals around the table are professionals who work alongside the child, the student's family, and many times, the student. Remembering this, you want them to hear the honest truth about the student's progress, but in a way that highlights strengths and focuses on the skill sets the team wants to enhance over the next year. You can do this through student-centered IEP writing. A *student-centered IEP* focuses on student abilities to help work on and through weaknesses, and goals are built around what a student *can* do. This allows the team to identify and leverage what a student can do to work on growing needed skills.

Here's an example:

Original sentence: "Amara cannot sit in her seat during academic instruction for more than two minutes."

Strengths-focused sentence: "At this time, Amara can independently sit in her seat during academic instruction for one and a half minutes."

A great exercise is to read the IEP with your mind set in the lens of the student. If your student read what you and the team wrote in the Present Levels, would the student be empowered? Or would they be heartbroken or feel ashamed?

Here's another example:

Original sentence: "Elijah does not interact with his peers."

Strengths-focused sentence: "At this time, Elijah engages with his peer through parallel play."

It is important that a team does not sugarcoat or diminish the needs your student has, but it is also important that you write an IEP as an empowering document focused on where the student is headed. As special education teachers, part of our job is to keep progress at the forefront and ensure that we are always advocating for the best possible future for our students. Keeping IEPs honest, clear, and strengths-focused is not the easiest of tasks, but one that is necessary.

Student Information

This section is typically the first page of an IEP. When it comes to the student information page, here are a few reminders:

- Make sure the student's first and last name are correct and spelled correctly. You may also want to add the student's nickname somewhere on this page if there's a spot, or you can put this information in the Present Levels.
- Make sure the student's date of birth is accurate. You may find it helpful to have the student's age displayed on this page too.
- Make sure the student's address is up to date and accurate.
- Ask the family to update the phone number on file, whether that is on the IEP or in the school's system. In this age of technology, it may be beneficial to ask for an updated email address too.
- Make sure the student's grade and school are correct and that the name of the child's homeroom or caseload teacher is on there too.
- Is the child's eligibility category listed somewhere? Is it correct, and does it need to be updated? You may also find it helpful to include the child's most recent eligibility date.
- What is the child's primary disability? Is it listed and correct? What about any secondary or tertiary disabilities? If these are not listed in the student information section, add them to the child's Present Levels.
- Make sure the triennial reevaluation date is correct as well as the next annual IEP date.
- Sometimes on this page you will see a spot for the student's anticipated date of graduation.

Depending on the IEP format your school uses, you may find the IEP team and participants listed, along with their roles. Make sure the participants' list is correct and everyone's name is spelled correctly, and that each participant's role is assigned or written by their name. Check to make sure that the IEP team is full, meaning make sure that the team aligns with the IDEA in terms of who should be there. If any contact information is shown here for IEP team participants, make sure the information is accurate.

The student information page contains a lot of very valuable and important information. It is vital for teachers to make sure that this page is accurate and up to date.

Present Levels of Academic and Functional Performance

This is the section of the IEP that provides a basis on which future instructional and educational services are determined and the baseline from which progress is measured.

The Present Levels of Academic and Functional Performance section of the IEP goes by many different names: PLOP, PLEP, PLAAFP, Present Ed Levels, and Present Levels.

IDEA has this to say about the Present Levels of Academic and Functional Performance in Section 1414(d):

- "The term 'individualized education program' or 'IEP' means a written statement for each child with a disability that is developed, reviewed, and revised in accordance with this section and that includes:
  - (I) a statement of the child's present levels of academic achievement and functional performance, including:
    - (aa) how the child's disability affects the child's involvement and progress in the general education curriculum;

- (bb) for preschool children, as appropriate, how the disability affects the child's participation in appropriate activities; and
- (cc) for children with disabilities who take alternate assessments aligned to alternate achievement standards, a description of benchmarks or short-term objectives. . . ."

Think about it this way: the Present Levels is your meat and potatoes. It is the section of the IEP that you should work on first. Once you have a solid Present Levels filled with all the data, the rest of the IEP falls into place and will leave breadcrumbs for all of the other decisions you'll make during the IEP process.

But what data and information should be written into the Present Levels? There are generally 14 different sections within the Present Levels that need to be addressed. Depending on the IEP writing system you're using, you may see one large, empty box to type in or multiple smaller boxes. Regardless, you will want to make sure the following information is included in the Present Levels.

Some IEP writing systems have the Present Levels broken down into their own sections and formatting.

Student Information

This may seem like a reiteration of the front page of the child's IEP, but you will want to make sure to include any pertinent student information, including the child's nickname, preferences, interests, strengths, and needs. You can list the child's most recent evaluation date, eligibility category, and the student's disability or disabilities. Include any medical concerns, including medications (as appropriate), health issues, and information about the student's attendance. Next, list the child's grades from the last year in any classes the child is or was enrolled in. A statement about how a student was graded may also be helpful, especially if the student was graded using a rubric. Additional data sources that you can include in the Present Levels might be attendance records, checklists, observational data, student work, behavior and/or disciplinary record data, progress monitoring data from the last year, and any state or district assessment data.

Family Concerns and Goals

Before you begin listing your evaluation and testing data, it is vital to include a section in the Present Levels about the family's concerns and a vision statement from the family and the child, as appropriate. This is one of the most overlooked, yet crucial steps in effectively writing collaborative IEPs. The parent input statement is how parents voice their concerns and priorities for their child, and it is more than one or two sentences. Ask clarifying questions to assist parents in developing their input statement, which in turn will help drive the team's decision making for IEP goals and services. Refer to Chapter 5 for more information on parent collaboration and to Chapter 1 for more on student involvement in the IEP process.

Testing and Evaluation Information

Now you'll list any testing and evaluation information, including the student's participation in the state's test, school benchmarks, and the most recent evaluation findings. If the student is new to special education, the evaluation data will come from the initial evaluation for eligibility. If this is an annual or amendment IEP, the evaluation data can come from any formal or informal assessments performed throughout the year, as well as information from the student's most recent evaluation or reevaluation. See Figure 3.1.

Here are four different types of assessments based on the response required by the child:

- **Selected Response** assessments require the student to produce evidence of learning by selecting a correct response from a set number of choices. These assessments measure knowledge acquisition.

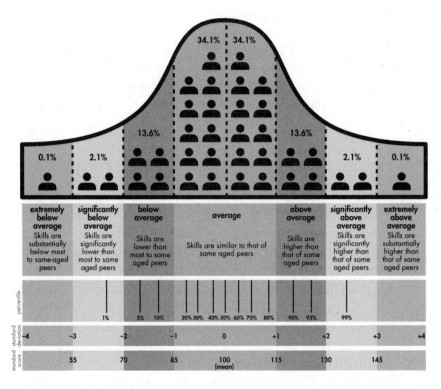

Figure 3.1 Understanding the Bell Curve Can Help an IEP Team Understand What a Student's Test or Evaluation Scores Mean in Relation to the Child's Peers.

- **Extended Written Response** assessments require a student to produce evidence of learning through a written response to a question or task. These types of assessments require students to apply reasoning and problem-solving skills in order to respond.
- **Performance** assessments require students to produce evidence or learning through creating or developing a product or performance. This type of assessment illuminates a student's skills, conceptual understandings, execution, and process abilities, and the student's ability to apply knowledge and skills.
- **Personal Communication** assessments require students to produce evidence of learning by speaking or writing.

Remember that *academic achievement* refers to a child's performance in any academic area. *Functional performance* refers to a child's performance in any area that is non-academic. These activities are often activities of daily living.

Additional areas to include in a child's Present Levels include:

- **Reading and Language Arts, Written Language, and Mathematics:** Add any testing information, how the student performs next to neurotypical, same-aged peers in their grade level, and any supports the student has received that did or did not work.
- **Communication:** The speech and language pathologist will more than likely fill in the majority of this information, but you as the teacher will want to add information as well. This is also where you would put any information about assistive technology and devices the child may utilize at school and at home to communicate wants and needs.
- **Motor Skills (Gross Motor and Fine Motor):** This is where the occupational therapist or physical therapist will fill in their information, but it's also important to add more information and data from the rest of the IEP team.
- **Social Skills:** Questions to ask yourself when writing this section of the Present Levels: what social skills does the child have or need to work on? Does the student have friends? How does the child interact with peers and adults? Are there developmental milestones the student needs to work toward?
- **Emotional Regulation:** How does the child respond to different situations at school?
- **Behavior:** What behaviors does the child exhibit while at school? What about behaviors exhibited at home? Does the child have a behavior plan? Was a Functional Behavior Assessment (FBA) conducted? If yes, when was it conducted and what were the FBA results?

- **Attention:** Does the child exhibit appropriate attention skills? Does the child need any supports or breaks? How long is the child's attention span for a preferred activity? What about during a non-preferred activity? What supports is the child currently receiving and using, and how are they working?
- **Vocational Skills:** What is the child or family's vision statement and what vocational skills are necessary for the child to prepare for further education, employment, and independent living?
- **Adaptive, Daily Living Skills, Independent Functioning:** This section of the Present Levels could cover a lot! Think about the child's self-help skills, self-advocacy, functional skills, and so on.
- **Health (including Vision and Hearing):** What are the most recent health evaluation results? Does the child wear glasses? Does the child wear hearing aids or have a cochlear implant? What supports or accommodations is the child currently receiving and how are they working?

Previous IEP Progress

You may also find it beneficial to add progress toward the child's previous IEP goals. A quick synopsis of the child's progress reports or a breakdown of which IEP goals were mastered and which were not can be very helpful in determining what IEP goals should be written next. Share what supports, interventions, and activities have been effective over the last year, and support families to be strong and effective advocates by sharing the knowledge, resources, and strategies discovered over the years. All of this data helps provide a baseline for this annual IEP.

You can also add more to this as needed for each individual student—for example, related services information and data.

Adverse Effects

To be eligible for an IEP, the child's disability must have an adverse effect on the child's educational performance. This means there must be a direct relationship between the child's disability and the child's academic performance in the general education classroom. Your impact statement describes how the student's disability is impacting their learning of grade-level content and standards.

For example:

Kenny has a specific learning disability that keeps him from accessing the 1st-grade general education curriculum.	Kenny's specific learning disability impacts his learning in mathematics and English, language arts. He has difficulty identifying and representing whole numbers to 20 and counting back from a given number. He is unable to retell text in a sequential order and struggles with decoding regularly spelled one-syllable words.

Which of these has a bigger impact that dictates adverse effects? The impact statement on the right is what to strive for. It is specific and lets anyone who reads Kenny's IEP know how his disability affects his educational performance.

Here are a few questions to think about when writing your impact statement:

- How will the child's deficits and/or struggles with this content area affect the child's learning?
- What will the child be unable to do without specific goals in this area?
- How will the child struggle in/with the general education grade level curriculum without specific instruction in this area?
- What are the student's challenges related to the disability?
- How will these challenges affect day-to-day life?

Now that you have a strongly written Present Levels section with a powerful impact statement, it's time to determine and write your IEP goals and objectives.

IEP Goals and Objectives

The IDEA does not specify how to write IEP goals, what subjects to cover, how many goals to include, or how to implement and measure them. But IEP goals are the heart of an IEP, and goals form the basis from which instruction, interventions, and services are determined.

Put another way, IEP goals are statements that describe what a student will achieve as a result of specific instruction, interventions, supports, and services. But how do you determine what to write IEP goals for? The IDEA does have this to say about IEP goals in Section 1414(d):

- "(II) a statement of measurable annual goals, including academic and functional goals, designed to:
  - (aa) meet the child's needs that result from the child's disability to enable the child to be involved in and make progress in the general education curriculum; and
  - (bb) meet each of the child's other educational needs that result from the child's disability. . . ."

Determining What IEP Goals to Write

Your starting point for choosing IEP goals is the Present Levels. Everything written outside of the Present Levels section of the IEP is determined by the information and data written in the Present Levels. A really strongly written Present Level section will guide you and leave breadcrumbs throughout the rest of the IEP to aid in data-driven decision making.

If a student has a significant area of need and the team has data to back this up, an IEP goal should be written for that area of need.

A student's IEP goals should be developed ambitiously in light of the child's circumstances. This means, too, that you should have a good baseline from which to build the student's IEP goals. And remember, all of that baseline data comes from the student's Present Levels.

You'll also need to look at what is being taught in the general education classroom. From there, you then have to figure out how to include the child appropriately in the general education curriculum and aligning a student's IEP goals with that grade's standards. An IEP goal should not be a restatement of the general education curriculum or a grade-level standard, and it should not be a list of expectations across all curriculum areas. A lot of your students' IEP goals will be aligned to content standards through prerequisite skills, so start to think more in terms of what skills the student needs to learn to master the curriculum's content. Your annual goals will guide your instruction for that student too.

> When determining IEP goals, it is also equally important to ask the parent, and the student, what their long-term vision is for the student! Remember: further education, employment, and independent living. You should think beyond the annual IEP when determining IEP goals too.

How to Write an IEP Goal

IEP goals can cover a very wide variety of skills, and you want all IEP goals to be SMART goals. SMART goals are specific, measurable, attainable, results-oriented or relevant, and time bound:

- **Specific:** The goal is specific in naming the skill or subject area and the targeted result.
- **Measurable:** The goal is stated in a way that the student's progress can be measured. Goals are typically measured through mastery criteria.

- **Attainable:** The goal needs to be realistic for the child to master for the duration of this IEP.
- **Results-oriented or relevant:** The goal specifically states what the child must do to accomplish it and the goal is relevant to the child.
- **Time bound:** The goal has a timeframe set for when the child will achieve the goal. This directly relates to when and how progress will be measured.

Specific: Aligning IEP Goals to State Standards

You may work in a school that requires your student IEP goals to be standards-aligned. This can seem overwhelming and it can be a little difficult, especially when a student is a few grade levels below their neurotypical peers. How do you write an IEP goal about a 3D object's circumference when the child is working on identifying 2D shapes? The first thing you want to do is think about the skill in a vertical alignment or spiral perspective; think prerequisite skills. Some states may provide this spiral for you, especially for alternate standards and alternate state test takers, but you can also determine what skill comes before or next by looking at your state's content standards.

For example: Let's say Tiana is a 3rd-grade student and has a documented need in mathematics, and she needs an IEP goal that is aligned with the 3rd-grade standard for identifying decisions involving income, spending, saving, credit, and charitable giving. But Tiana is not yet able to accomplish this 3rd-grade-level state standard.

Your first step is to look at the data to see what the baseline says. In relation to this standard, what prerequisite skills does the child already have? And what other prerequisite skills does the child need to meet this grade level standard, or skill?

Let's continue with the example:

Tiana is able to identify coins and bills, can count mixed coins to $1, and can count bills of the same dollar amount to $100. She can skip count by 1, 2, 5, 10, and 20 to 100. She is able to add whole numbers to 100 with regrouping and subtract whole numbers within

100 without regrouping. Her baseline data shows that she currently is able to write a cent value to describe a coin or bill with 95% mastery, and she is able to make change with mixed bills and coins when trying to purchase items or pay for a service with 10% accuracy.

If the state standard is *identifying decisions involving income, spending, saving, credit, and charitable giving*, and Tiana's peers are learning this standard in terms of goods and services, and also the benefits of saving for planned and unplanned expenses, writing an IEP goal for making change when trying to purchase items or pay for a service seems to adequately meet the requirements. Tiana will not be able to perform the grade-level standard without this prerequisite skill, and because she is able to add and subtract whole numbers and identify coins and bills, this may be the best suited next IEP goal for her at this time.

But you could also write an IEP goal for counting mixed coins and bills to a specific number due to her current mastery levels of the prerequisite skills. The final step in determining which prerequisite skill to write an IEP goal for is prioritizing what skills the student will need for "further education, employment, and independent living," but also what skills the parent and team want to prioritize in this IEP. Essentially you want to know what the prerequisite skills are for the grade level standards, and working backward is the best way to dig into writing this type of IEP goal for your students.

Measurable: Determining the Criteria of an IEP Goal

IEP goals need to have a criteria that specifies how the student will achieve success or mastery. The criteria you choose needs to identify how well the student needs to perform the skill and over what period of time the student must perform the skill in order for it to be considered mastered.

When it comes to measuring how well the student performs a skill, you can measure that in terms of the following:

- Accuracy.
- Frequency.
- Duration.
- Rate.

- Distance.
- Intensity.
- Latency.

Accuracy

Accuracy is measured as a percentage, and this mastery criteria will be different for every skill that you teach.

It is also best practice to not use "80% accuracy" all of the time. For example, if you are teaching a child to count from 1 to 20, you want and need the student to know every single number all of the time (this is a foundational skill!). It will not be a mastered skill if the child skips multiple numbers as they're counting, and the child will not be able to master higher level skills without this base of knowledge. So you know, for this skill, the mastery criteria must be 100%. But there are times when it is more appropriate for a child's mastery criteria to be 20% or 50%. To determine the mastery criteria, you must also look at the child's baseline data. For more about using data to choose IEP goals, refer to Chapter 2.

Frequency

Frequency is the number of times something occurs, and is generally measured in trials. Frequency data collected on a behavior will show the number of times a behavior occurred during a specific time period.

For example, if you are teaching a student to look both ways and cross the street safely, you also need the student to perform this skill correctly all of the time, or to 100% accuracy. If you made your mastery criteria two out of three times, then that means the child would still master the skill if they didn't cross the street safely a few times. No way! You need that mastery criteria to be 100%, or 10 out of 10 trials.

Duration

Duration is used in terms of time. For example, a student will do X for five minutes. When using this criteria to measure behavior, duration data reflects the amount of time the behavior occurs.

Rate

Rate is how quickly something occurs within a given timeframe.

Distance

Distance is used to measure a distance. For example, the student will independently propel themself in their wheelchair for 15 feet.

Intensity

Intensity is collected using a scale to show feelings or emotions, or collect data on the intensity of a behavior that occurs.

Latency

Latency is the measurement of time between two behaviors, usually the time between the antecedent (what occurs before the behavior) and the behavior or a directive and compliance.

If you feel a student needs some additional supports built in to their mastery criteria, you can:

1. Add prompts to your goals and objectives. Have the student's yearly goal show that they will complete the task independently with 100% accuracy, and their objectives can include completing the task with 100% accuracy, but with three verbal prompts. This allows that 100% accuracy to still be the focus, but with support as they learn to do this independently. Again, this is all variable on what the skill is.
2. Double up on criteria. You will notice accuracy and frequency criteria used together a lot. *The student will . . . with 48% accuracy in three of four consecutive trials.*

A student has truly mastered a skill when they are able to execute it successfully across multiple environments, and with different materials and people. This is known as generalization of a skill, and what you should strive for in measuring student skill mastery. So keep it clear and ensure that mastery criteria really does show complete skill mastery. When you write IEP goals using the correct criteria for the skill, your data collection method will naturally follow. You can learn more about data collection in Chapter 2.

Attainable and Relevant: Adding Functional IEP Goals

You already know that IEPs are all-encompassing and they look at the whole child, and you know that teaching and learning are more than academics. There are multiple sections in the Present Levels that help you cover more than that, which includes functional skills. You have and use functional skills daily, but some of your students may need to be explicitly taught functional skills. Each student on your caseload may need to be taught a different functional skill. It is variable and dependent on the student's needs and the parent's vision statement for the student. Functional skills are skills that an individual needs to live as independently as possible. Think of ADLs (Activities of Daily Living). Functional skills can be communication, choice-making, social skills, safety, self-care, life skills, leisure, recreation, vocational skills, community-based learning, functional academics, time management, and more. You can take these skills and align functional skills with academic standards and your IEP goals.

> IEPs are "designed to meet a [student's] unique needs and prepare them for further education, employment, and independent living."[1]

Here are a few examples:

Standards: Measurement, addition, elapsed time.
Potential Functional Academic IEP Goal: cooking.
Standards: Listening and speaking.
Potential Functional Academic IEP Goal: Conversations on the phone or with peers, calling to make a doctor's appointment.
Standard: Money.
Potential Functional Academic IEP Goal: Paying for a service, shopping, budgeting.

There are a lot of variables in determining IEP goals, and it really comes down to determinations made by the IEP team based on the data presented in the Present Levels. But start with the

Present Levels and the vision statement, then discuss how you can turn the standard or skill into something more functional for the student.

How Many IEP Goals Should a Student Have?

If you find yourself with a large list of student needs to write IEP goals for, it's time to prioritize the skills from within the child's needs. There is no set number of goals an IEP can or should have, but best practice is to think about what is attainable for that child. Think realistically about how many skills can be worked on in the classroom setting during each marking period (with data collection in mind) without overwhelming the child or the child's teacher.

Yes, you want to address all of a student's needs—and you will—but in order to implement the IEP with fidelity, you have to start with skills that the IEP team has determined are high priority. And, just like how no two IEPs are the same, a prioritized list of skills will be different for each student.

Time Bound: Progress Measurement of IEP Goals

For all students who have an IEP, you have to write into the IEP how progress toward IEP goal mastery will be measured and when this progress will be relayed. The IDEA says an IEP must include:

- "(III) a description of how the child's progress toward meeting the annual goals described in subclause (II) will be measured and when periodic reports on the progress the child is making toward meeting the annual goals (such as through the use of quarterly or other periodic reports, concurrent with the issuance of report cards) will be provided. . . ."

As Chapter 2 explains, data can be collected in a variety of ways, and it can be collected through many different evaluation procedures, including but not limited to:

- Observations.
- Written or oral tests and reports.
- Work samples.
- Teacher-made tests.
- Criterion-referenced tests.
- Checklists.
- Behavior charting.
- Time samples.
- Comprehensive evaluations and assessments.

The easiest way to write a SMART goal is to have a formula to fill in the blanks with the essential information, as shown in Figure 3.2.

IEP Goal Formula #1 THE INTENTIGNAL IEP

Given	Student will	with	with	as measured by
		accuracy	supports	

IEP Goal Formula #2 THE INTENTIGNAL IEP

By	Student will	in	as measured by	with	with
		setting		accuracy	supports

IEP Goal Formula #3 THE INTENTIGNAL IEP

Audience (who will perform the task)	Behavior (what is the observable act or behavior)	Condition (what is the relevant condition under which the student is expected to perform the desired behavior)	Degree (what is the degree or criteria for the student to demonstrate achievement of the behavior)	Expected Date (what is the expected date the goal will be met)

Figure 3.2 Write Smart Goals Using This Formula to Fill in the Blanks with the Essential Information.

IEP Objectives and Benchmarks

IEP goals are the overall target for a skill by a set time. Goals are driven by what the student needs, which is written in the Present Levels, and are S.M.A.R.T. in nature. They explain exactly what the outcome should be based on the student's needs, how it will be measured and achieved, and when it will be accomplished by. It is where the student should be by the next annual IEP meeting. Goals are essentially the backbone of the IEP and provide the IEP team with an end outcome in mind for that skill's mastery.

Most, not all, IEP goals are supported with objectives. The best analogy is to think of a staircase. The annual IEP goal is the overarching skill that you are working toward. Each step of the staircase is an objective, or a baby step to get your student to the top, or mastery of the annual IEP goal. The objectives support the goals by providing clear parts, or steps, to reach that end result. While objectives are not always required (this determination is left up to the states), they are especially useful for complex goals. Objectives break down the steps of those complex and larger IEP goals so that students can make clear progress in an organized, step-by-step fashion. In other words, the objectives provide tiers that the student should accomplish in order to achieve the larger IEP goal, which then serve as progress monitoring points.

The Difference between Objectives and Benchmarks

You may hear the term *objective* and *benchmark* thrown around interchangeably, but truly they are different when it comes to IEPs. And when I say different, I mean in terms of how they build on one another, how many you might write under an IEP goal— not in a way that the objective or benchmark is not a SMART goal. While they may be written differently, both objectives and benchmarks are the smaller, more manageable goals a student works to master, and they are derived from the annual IEP goal. Think back to the staircase analogy. The easiest way for me to explain the difference between an objective and a benchmark is to show you examples.

Important Legal Information to Know about IEP Goals

One point I want you to remember is that while the IDEA does outline many regulations you must follow, many things are left up to the states and school districts to implement further. PL 108-446 from within the IDEA reauthorization is a great example. This section of the law states that short-term objectives only need to be written for students who take alternative assessments. But—and this is why it is important to know your state laws and regulations—the majority of IEPs written include short-term objectives. This is because the U.S. Department of Education has allowed states to include short-term objectives in IEPs for students who do not take alternative assessments, at the state's discretion.

IEP Objectives

Objectives should not match your annual IEP goal. Instead, an objective should provide students with the supports they need in order to reach mastery. Objectives usually build on one other in either skill level or prerequisite skills. Another way to think about objectives is that they break down the skill into necessary steps or smaller skills that make up the larger skill.

For example:

Annual IEP Goal: By the end of Quarter 4, when given addition and subtraction problems within 50, student will draw a picture to help them complete the problems, in three out of four trials with 70% accuracy.

1. By the end of Quarter 1, when presented with the name of a number between 1 and 50 in verbal or written format, student will point to identify the correct number in number format in written form with 50% accuracy in three of four trials.

2. By the end of Quarter 2, given visual, verbal, and tactile cues, student will use one-to-one correspondence to count objects up to 50 independently in three out of four trials with 50% accuracy.
3. By the end of Quarter 3, given visual supports and manipulatives, student will use manipulatives to perform single digit addition and subtraction with 50% accuracy in two of four trials.

IEP Benchmarks

Benchmarks are used to stack the skill, meaning the skill is built on each marking period, and in most cases you'll have three or four benchmarks under an IEP goal. Benchmarks are the major milestones that a student must demonstrate mastery of, which then leads up to the annual goal. With benchmarks, the topic or skill is the same, but you are modifying the criteria, supports, and level of the skill mastery.

For example:

Annual IEP Goal: Given a model and minimal prompting, the student will print 26 lowercase and 26 uppercase letters of the alphabet with 75% accuracy in three of four trials.

1. Given a model and verbal prompting, the student will print 13 lowercase letters of the alphabet with 75% accuracy in three of four trials.
2. Given a model and verbal prompting, the student will print 26 lowercase letters of the alphabet with 75% accuracy in two of four trials.
3. Given a model and verbal prompting, the student will print 13 uppercase letters of the alphabet, with 75% accuracy in three of four trials.

The key takeaways here of IEP goal writing are:

- The Present Level section will guide you in determining what IEP goals to write. It all starts here.
- All of your goals, objectives, and benchmarks need to be SMART.

- Objectives break down the annual goal into distinct skills that make up the larger skill. Benchmarks describe specific progress a student must make in a smaller amount of time. Your school will more than likely provide guidelines on which to write and how they would like them written.

Once you've written your IEP goals, it's time to determine what accommodations and modifications the student will need to help them learn and master those IEP goal skills.

Accommodations and Modifications

Before you can choose accommodations and modifications, it's important to know the difference between the two. An accommodation changes the course or test presentation, location, timing, student response, or other attribute that is necessary to provide access for the student to participate and demonstrate achievement. Accommodations preserve validity and do not alter or lower the standard or expectation. This means there is no change to the learning content. Modifications change the course or test presentation, location, timing, student response, or other attribute that is necessary to provide access for the student to participate and demonstrate achievement. Modifications do not preserve validity, but they do alter or lower the standard or expectation. This means there is a change to the content to meet the student's needs. When accommodations are not sufficient, are not working, or are not helping the student achieve success, that's when you begin using modifications. In easier terms, an accommodation changes *how* the student learns the material and a modification changes *what* the student is expected to learn.

Here are some examples of both:

- **Accommodations** include, but are certainly not limited to, large print text, reteaching concepts, working in pairs or small groups, using a calculator, extended time, and flexible seating.

- **Modifications** may include use of a different grading rubric, modifying the format of a test or activity, modifying the reading level, change of student expectations, and reduced complexity of an activity.

The Five Types of Learning Styles

- **Auditory:** Learns best by hearing the material.
- **Kinesthetic:** Learns best by doing or moving.
- **Multisensory:** Learns best by seeing, hearing, touching, and/or performing.
- **Tactile:** Learns best by touching the material.
- **Visual:** Learns best by seeing the material.

It is important to know that a student may have one or more learning styles, and through all of the team's evaluations, observations, and input, you as a team will determine the best route for lesson and instruction adaptations.

But how do you determine what accommodations and modifications to choose? Just like IEP goal-writing, it all goes back to the Present Levels. The data, observations, and input written into the Present Levels will guide you to what IEP goals to write, and your supports and services will help you achieve IEP goal mastery. So what supports does the student need to not only master this skill, but also learn and access grade level content? And how can you leverage the student's strengths and learning style to help them learn?

For example:

Present Levels: Ava is a 5th-grade student with a specific learning disability that enjoys reading and looking at books, and using technology. She is trustworthy, hardworking, resilient, and works well with a partner. She is currently reading two grade levels below her peers, but is a very quick reader, leading to struggles with reading comprehension. Ava is able to sequence a four-part story when provided with visuals, either pictorial or written representations.

Potential IEP Goal: Given text on her instructional level, Ava will evaluate details read to determine key ideas, citing evidence from the text to explain her thinking, with 65% accuracy in three of four trials.

Potential Accommodations and Modifications: Use of peer readers, provide study guides or guided notes, use of graphic organizers, highlight the most important parts of reading assignments, provide a summary of the text, stop for comprehension checks throughout text, provide a vocabulary list with definitions, modify the reading level of the text.

Ava may not need all of those accommodations or modifications, but based on her strengths, needs, and learning style, these may be options the team explores to help her learn grade-level content and work toward mastery of her IEP goal.

Suggesting Adaptions

Choosing the most appropriate accommodations and modifications is more than making a selection from a drop-down box or a predetermined list. This section of the IEP is crucial in making sure the student receives the supports needed to succeed and learn new skills. And when you break down the selection process, you are diving into the nine different types of adaptations. An adaptation is a change in your teaching process, materials, or assignments, or what the student is expected to produce to show learning. Accommodations and modifications are adaptations, and you can sort any accommodation or modification into one of the nine types of adaptations:[2]

- **Size:** Adapt the number of items the student is expected to learn or complete.

- **Time:** Adapt the time allotted and allowed for learning, task completion, or testing.
- **Level of Support:** Increase the amount of personal assistance with the student.
- **Input:** Adapt the way instruction is delivered to the student.
- **Output:** Adapt how the student can respond to instruction.
- **Difficulty:** Adapt the skill level, problem type, or the rules for how the student may approach the work.
- **Participation:** Adapt the extent to which the student is actively involved in the task.
- **Alternate Goals:** Adapt the goal or outcome expectations while using the same materials.
- **Substitute Curriculum:** Provide different instruction and materials to meet the student's individual goals.

The adaptations written into a student's IEP is where specially designed instruction, or SDI, comes in. PL 108-446 within the IDEA reauthorization defines *specially designed instruction* as:

"(3) Specially designed instruction means adapting, as appropriate to the needs of an eligible child under this part, the content, methodology, or delivery of instruction:

(i) To address the unique needs of the child that result from the child's disability; and
(ii) To ensure access of the child to the general curriculum, so that the child can meet the educational standards within the jurisdiction of the public agency that apply to all children."

SDI requires the team to adapt curriculum and content and the instructional delivery. This can come in many forms, it can look many ways, and it will be different for each of your students. You are also not altering the grade level content standards, you are altering the curriculum so the student can have equal access. What I want to emphasize here is that as a special education teacher and IEP team member you are already doing this—providing specially designed instruction—and you may not know the technical terminology, but you are doing it.

The Difference between SDI and Differentiation

Differentiation is used to give all students a chance to demonstrate learning in ways that work best for them. Differentiation is a method of teaching used with all students, whereas SDI is a method of teaching used to address individual goals and needs, and is based on the child's evaluation results and specific, individualized student needs. To learn more about SDI, visit Section 300.39 within the IDEA.[3]

Tailoring the Accommodations and Modifications

Before you move into Related Services, it is equally as important to remember that accommodations and modifications should be individualized. That doesn't mean that four or five of your students can't have the same exact accommodation, but it's important that when your students work with other adults and professionals, those adults and professionals know what each accommodation means and looks like for that specific student. This means the team must discuss who is implementing the accommodation or modification, what this accommodation or modification looks like when implemented for this student, and how the fidelity of its implementation will be monitored.

For example, in Ava's IEP, one of her accommodations the team discussed was "provide a summary of the text." If left unexplained, that accommodation can be translated in many different ways. For Ava, this accommodation might look like the teacher providing a written summary of the text in 10 sentences of less. But for William, this accommodation might look like a pictorial representation that sequences the events of the story. And maybe for Sebastian, the teacher is providing guided notes and a graphic organizer for

Sebastian to fill in while reading. Do you see how one accommodation can be interpreted multiple different ways? To prevent com-
promised implementation, you can write specifics into the child's
Present Levels, be more specific when writing out the child's accommodations, and write in teacher training into the IEP. By doing all
of these, you are protecting the fidelity of the child's supports.

Related Services

When it comes to related services, the IDEA says the IEP must
include:

- "(IV) a statement of the special education and related services
  and supplementary aids and services, based on peer-reviewed
  research to the extent practicable, to be provided to the child, or
  on behalf of the child, and a statement of the program modifications or supports for school personnel that will be provided for
  the child:
    - (aa) to advance appropriately toward attaining the annual
      goals;
    - (bb) to be involved in and make progress in the general educa-
      tion curriculum in accordance with subclause (I) and to partic-
      ipate in extracurricular and other nonacademic activities; and
    - (cc) to be educated and participate with other children with
      disabilities and nondisabled children in the activities described
      in this subparagraph . . . ."

"Related services means transportation and such developmental, corrective, and other supportive services as are required to assist
a child with a disability to benefit from special education . . .," and
Section 300.34 of the IDEA defines what *related service* means in
the IEP in more depth. Related services may include, but are not
limited to:

- Speech-language pathology.
- Audiology.

- Occupational therapy.
- Physical therapy.
- Counseling.
- Orientation and mobility.
- Assistive technology.
- Psychological services.
- School health and nurse services.
- Medical.
- Parent counseling and training.
- Social work.
- Interpreting services.
- Vision.
- Transportation.

Each related service listed in the student's IEP must include the related service type, frequency, duration, location, and the start and end dates of the service. *Related service type* refers to what the service is. *Frequency* refers to how often the service is provided. *Duration* refers to how long each service session will be. *Location* refers to where the service will be provided. *Start and end dates* refer to when the service will begin and end. Most times this aligns with the child's annual IEP dates. The IEP also needs to specify whether the services will be provided in small groups, whole groups, or 1:1 sessions. Many times, the service provider will come to the IEP meeting and have a consensus based on data and evaluations, how much time the student needs per week, month, or marking period to work toward mastery of the skills or tasks the service provider will provide.

For example: Camila receives counseling services two times per week for individual 15-minute sessions in the school psychologist's office, from August 2023 through February 2024.

Many of the students that you service in special education are also in need of medical services so that they can participate in their FAPE. But a larger question here arises, which medical services are covered under the law? It's important to note that if the service can be performed by someone other than a physician and does not involve a medical diagnosis or evaluation, the service should be included in the student's IEP. On the other hand, if the service requires a diagnosis or evaluation, the medical service has to be performed by a physician. This is a general guideline, as your state's policies may provide more direction on what this means for you and your students.

In 1984, the courts decided in *the Irving Independent School District v. Amber Tatro* case that a medical service that allows the child to benefit from special education is a supportive service that is required of schools.[4]

Extended School Year

Determining eligibility for Extended School Year (ESY), requires a review of progress monitoring data and a deep-dive conversation with the IEP team. ESY is not just for regression and recoupment, and ESY services are not relevant for only summer breaks. The following should be considered when making a determination for ESY eligibility:

- Regression and recoupment: is the child likely to lose critical skills or fail to recover these skills within a reasonable time?
- Degree of progress toward IEP goals and objectives.
- Emerging skills and breakthrough opportunities: is the student at a crucial stage in mastering a critical skill and a lapse in services will substantially limit the child's learning of the skill?
- Interfering behavior: does the child's behavior interfere with the child's ability to benefit from special education?

- Nature and/or severity of the child's disability: is the nature of severity of the student's disability such that the student will not receive a reasonable level of benefit from their education during the regular school year if ESY services are not provided?
- Special circumstances that interfere with the child's ability to benefit from special education: are there any extenuating circumstances that make it unlikely the student will receive FAPE without ESY services?

Not all students who have a disability will require ESY services, and the decision should not be based solely on the child's disability.

How is ESY different than summer school?

ESY services are provided to only students with IEPs, and the service's intensity, duration, and frequency are determined based on the child's IEP. Summer school is provided for all students for a predetermined amount of time set forth by the district, and the focus is to help students meet the grade-level standards in their state.

Special Factors

The Special Factors section of an IEP includes a couple of very important checkboxes and information on testing as related to the IEP. Testing in this section is related to any state testing the student may take in the annual IEP year or benchmark assessments the school will provide. See Figure 3.3.

This is what the IDEA has to say about testing in Section 300.160 and Section 1412(a)(16):[5]

"A State must ensure that all children with disabilities are included in all general State and district-wide assessment programs . . . with appropriate accommodations and alternate assessments, if necessary, as indicated in their respective IEPs.

Special Factors Checklist

Y   N

☐   ☐   Does the child have behavior that impedes his or her learning or the learning of others?

☐   ☐   Does the child have limited English proficiency?

☐   ☐   Is the child blind or visually impaired?

☐   ☐   Does the child require accessible alternate format versions of textbooks or instructional materials due to a documented disability?

☐   ☐   Does the child have communication needs?

☐   ☐   Does the child need assistive technology devices and/or services?

☐   ☐   Does the child require specially designed physical education?

☐   ☐   Will the child participate in statewide testing?

☐   ☐   Does the child require benchmarks/short-term objectives aligned to alternate achievement standards?

Figure 3.3   The Special Factors Checklist

(16) Participation in assessments

- (A) All children with disabilities are included in all general State and district wide assessment programs, including assessments described under section 6311 of this title, with appropriate accommodations and alternate assessments where necessary and as indicated in their respective individualized education programs.
- (B) Accommodation guidelines: The State (or, in the case of a districtwide assessment, the local educational agency) has developed guidelines for the provision of appropriate accommodations.
- (C) Alternate assessments
  - (i) The State (or, in the case of a districtwide assessment, the local educational agency) has developed and implemented guidelines for the participation of children with disabilities in alternate assessments for those children who cannot

participate in regular assessments under subparagraph (A) with accommodations as indicated in their respective individualized education programs.

- (ii) Requirements for alternate assessments. The guidelines under clause (i) shall provide for alternate assessments that:
  - (I) are aligned with the challenging State academic content standards under section 6311(b)(1) of this title and alternate academic achievement standards under section 6311(b)(1) (E) of this title; and
  - (II) if the State has adopted alternate academic achievement standards permitted under section 6311(b)(1)(E) of this title, measure the achievement of children with disabilities against those standards."

Essentially, what all of this means is the IEP needs to answer these two questions:

- If the child participates in the assessment, how?
- If they do not participate, why not, and what alternate assessment will be used instead?

State Testing

Children with disabilities must participate in their state's grade-level assessments to determine their level of content mastery, just as their peers without disabilities must participate, unless a child's IEP team determines that a given assessment is not appropriate for the student. The IDEA permits children with disabilities to participate in large-scale assessment programs with accommodations. Those accommodations are individually determined for a given child by their IEP team, and the accommodation a child receives is based on an individual consideration of that child's needs, as determined by the child's IEP team.

Accommodations chosen for testing should be similar to the accommodations a student receives in the classroom. Many accommodations allowed for state testing fall into any of the four categories: presentation, response, setting, and time and scheduling. For some states, only specific accommodations are permitted for state testing, so be sure to check your state's Department of Education website.

Alternate Testing

If the IEP team determines that it is inappropriate for a child to participate in the state or school's assessment, even with accommodations, the child can take the alternate assessment. When this determination is made, the team must write a statement into the child's IEP that explains why this is appropriate for this student.

The IDEA requires each state to develop and implement at least one alternate assessment, unless all students can be assessed through the general assessment. Most alternate assessments are based on grade-level academic achievement standards, modified academic achievement standards, or alternate academic achievement standards.

Transition Services

Transition services must be addressed no later than the first IEP that will be in effect when the child turns 16, according to the IDEA, and in some states it is earlier. The transition services must be updated annually with the child's annual IEP, and it is important that IEP teams begin planning for a student's lifelong outcomes. The student is the heart of the IEP and, as such, the heart of the transition plan. This plan prepares the student for a successful future with as much independence as possible.

IEPs are written to plan for a student's "further education, employment, and independent living," so you should be thinking about transition services before the child hits transition age in your state.

Transition planning focuses attention on how the student's secondary schooling can be planned to help the student make a successful transition to life after high school. According to the IDEA in Section 300.43,[6] the IEP must include:

- Appropriate measurable postsecondary goals based upon age-appropriate transition assessments related to training, education, employment, and where appropriate, independent living skills.
- The transition services, including courses of study, need to assist the student with a disability in reaching those goals, which is typically made through a statement of transition services.

The statement of transition services should identify and help the team plan for the student's educational coursework that the student will be taking after becoming 16, or younger in some states. This statement also needs to include a few key components. An IEP must include transition services and activities in the following areas, as they align with statement of responsibilities of the district, and when applicable, any participating agencies that may be providing provisions of services and activities:

- **Instruction:** Any instruction or specific courses that the student might need to prepare for independent living.
- **Related services:** Any related services that a student may need as a transitional service to support the student in attaining projected life outcomes.
- **Employment and other adult living objectives:** Any services or activities the student needs to prepare for employment and to assist the student in meeting other adult living objectives (e.g., interview skills).
- **Community living experiences:** Indicate if a student needs to participate in any community-based experiences or learn to access community resources to achieve their projected adult outcomes.
- **Activities of daily living (ADLs),** if appropriate: Services or activities that will assist the student in ADLs (e.g., dressing, hygiene, self-care, and self-medication).

- **Functional vocational assessment,** if appropriate: This is an assessment to determine the student's strengths, abilities, and needs in an actual or simulated work setting or in real or simulated work experiences.

Transition Frameworks, Curriculum, and Assessments

When it comes to planning for the transition section of an IEP, it may be helpful to use a framework that focuses on the student. Here are a few frameworks that may be helpful to you and your IEP teams:

- Making Action Plans.
- Planning Alternative Tomorrows of Hope.
- Person-Centered Planning.

Transition curriculum:

- Council for Exceptional Children's Life Centered Career Education (LCCE).

Transition assessments:

- Enderle-Severson Transition Rating Scale.
- BRIGANCE Employability Inventory of Essential Skills.

Additional resources:

- Transition Coalition.
- National Technical Assistance Center on Transition: The Collaborative.
- National Center on Secondary Education and Transition (NCSET).

Developing Transition Plans

There are a number of opportunities and programs available for students preparing to exit high school. Although each transition plan and IEP must be individualized, the IEP team can use existing resources for ideas and strategies. It is essential that you, along with family and the student, examine numerous programs and options to prepare a student for their desired post-school endeavors. Opportunities you can guide students and families toward include, but are not limited to:

- Paid employment.
- Community-based work experiences.
- Internships.
- Mentorships.
- Apprenticeship programs.
- Career pathways.

You also want the transition plan to align with the student's vision statement and goals, while also writing a plan that assists with the student in achieving their projected adulthood outcomes. The transition plan needs to be outcome-oriented and promote movement of the student from high school to lifetime activities, and it should align with the family and the student's vision statement. Lifetime activities can include anything that aligns with the student's postsecondary goals, including:

- Postsecondary education.
- Vocational training.
- Employment.
- Continuing and adult education.
- Adult services.
- Independent living.
- Community participation.

When you are navigating a family through the transition phase of life, it is important to engage in conversations about what is possible for the student. Provide your families with examples of how their child's strengths and mastered skills open opportunities, and share what the family can expect as they continue down this new path. Listen to your family's concerns, goals, and expectations, and provide them with ample information throughout the transition process. The connections you help build and foster will set the student up for lifelong success as an adult.

Age of Majority and the Transfer of Rights

When the student reaches the age of majority, age 18 or younger in some states, the IEP must include a statement that the student has been informed of their rights under the IDEA about the age of majority and the transfer of rights. This means that when a student reaches the age of majority, the year before this, the student must be informed of their rights. When the student reaches the age of majority, the IEP team has to meet a few components to comply with the IDEA. To be in compliance according to Section 300.520, the team must:

- Provide and send notice to the family and the student.
- Discuss the rights to be transferred with the student.
- Record the date the student and the family were notified.
- Maintain a copy of the notifications sent to the student and the family.
- Review records and legal documents, as necessary.

Determining the Least Restrictive Environment and Placement

By this point in the IEP writing process, you have written the rest of the IEP document. It's all led up to this—what will the child's Least Restrictive Environment (LRE) be? This is also called the placement. The LRE refers to the setting in which instruction and interventions occur, and is a continuum of services, ranging from the general education classroom setting to a hospital placement or the child's home. The IEP team determines the extent to which the student will be educated with their peers.

The student's disability should not be a factor in determining LRE, and placement should not be determined by space available at the school, the type of classroom, the building the student attends, the student's IQ or behaviors, or any available funding or lack thereof. The topic of placement should be the final discussion at the IEP meeting. See Figure 3.4.

LRE guarantees a student's right to be educated in the setting provided to same-aged, nondisabled peers, given appropriate

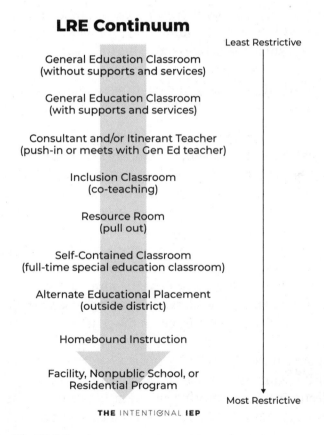

LRE Continuum

Least Restrictive

General Education Classroom
(without supports and services)

General Education Classroom
(with supports and services)

Consultant and/or Itinerant Teacher
(push-in or meets with Gen Ed teacher)

Inclusion Classroom
(co-teaching)

Resource Room
(pull out)

Self-Contained Classroom
(full-time special education classroom)

Alternate Educational Placement
(outside district)

Homebound Instruction

Facility, Nonpublic School, or
Residential Program

Most Restrictive

THE INTENTIǴNAL IEP

Figure 3.4   The LRE Continuum

supports to help the disabled student be successful in that setting. Again, LRE is a continuum of services, and the law requires that IEP teams consider the general education classroom setting first. Deciding on a more restrictive environment, like special classes or schools, requires the IEP team to document the evidence reviewed that demonstrates the need for the student to be in the more restrictive setting.

LRE Components

There are three basic components to LRE:

- Disabled students should have access to and be involved in the general education curriculum.
- Disabled students should be educated with their nondisabled peers.
- A continuum of services and environments should be provided to meet the needs of individual students.

In order to determine a child's placement, you have to consider the family's vision for the student, the student's interests and strengths, the supports and services needed, and information about the general education curriculum. Then, you have to look at the total percentage of special education services provided inside of the general education setting, and this is calculated based on the amount of time the student spends in the general education classroom. It is important to not include any services provided in the general education setting in the special education time section of the formula. This includes any consultations or any services listed in the supplementary aids section of the IEP that the student receives in the general education setting.

LRE Formula

Depending on the IEP writing program you use, this percentage may be determined for you based on the service minutes put into the IEP writing system by the team, but let's take a look at the LRE Formula broken down into steps.

The LRE Formula:

- **Step 1** is to calculate the total minutes of service the student receives in the special education setting. To do this, you add the student's minutes of special education service and related services that are provided outside of the general education setting.
- **Step 2** is to calculate the total number of minutes in the general education setting. To do this, you subtract the total number of special education minutes from the total number of instructional minutes per week.
- **Step 3** is to calculate the percentage of minutes the student receives in the general education setting. Divide the number of minutes in the general education setting by the total number of instructional minutes per week.
- **Step 4** is to multiply this number by 100, or move the decimal two spots to the right. You will then round this number to the nearest whole percent number.
- **Step 5** is to determine, based on your district's continuum of services, where the student's needs fall.

It is important to note that a student's LRE can change at any time. For example, Veronica's LRE in elementary school might be different than when she goes to middle school. Daniel's LRE may need to be updated mid-year due to behavioral needs. Sutton might be making strides and may need to be placed in a general education classroom with supports and services, instead of the resource room setting. When determining a student's LRE, it is important to remember that a student does not need to have the ability to master the grade level curriculum and content in order to be included in the general education classroom setting. Even if it might be a challenge for the student, the benefits will far outweigh the negatives.

Questions to Ask about the LRE

The LRE is the environment that is most conducive to instruction in the desired skills, provided additional supports and services are in that environment. Here are six questions you can use to help you assess the LRE:

- Can an appropriate education in the general education classroom with the use of supplementary aids and services be achieved satisfactorily?
- If the student is placed in a more restrictive setting, is the student included to the "maximum extent appropriate"?
- What are the educational benefits of this setting?
- What are the non-academic benefits?
- What effect will the student with a disability have on the teacher and their peers?
- What will the supplementary services cost in order for the student to stay in the inclusive setting?

The data will dictate the best placement for the child, and it is the IEP team's duty to make sure the student's placement is accurate and appropriate.

Transfer IEPs

IEPs must be reviewed annually at a minimum, and you can make amendments, or revisions, at any time. But what happens when a student transfers in from another district or state? Regardless of when a child transfers into your school, the receiving district must provide comparable services to those in the sending district's IEP until they develop and implement a new IEP. In some cases, a new evaluation for the child may need to take place as well before a new IEP can be written and implemented.

As a teacher, it is really hard to write an IEP about a student you don't know yet, and also for a student whom you don't have any data on. Here's what I recommend.

- Have a conversation with the parent.
  - Let them know your concerns. Ask for their input and any additional documentation they may have. Share your plan for collecting as much data as possible. The parent will appreciate this.
  - Provide the parent with district special education information and any contact information they may need to keep on hand (administration, extracurriculars, transportation, community, etc.). Remember, use the resources available to your student's benefit.
- Schedule time on your calendar in the days leading up to the IEP's due date to collect data. Enlist the help of your paraprofessionals and fellow IEP team members to collect data as well.
- Schedule time on your calendar to write the IEP.

Prior Written Notice

Prior Written Notice, or PWN, is meant to provide documentation of decisions made by the IEP team, namely, the Local Education Agency, or LEA. It's intended to give the family adequate notice before a decision is implemented. An LEA cannot make placement decisions or any other IEP decisions prior to an IEP meeting; this is considered predetermination. According to Section 303.421 of the IDEA,[7] the purpose of a PWN is to:

- Provide comprehensive documentation of the proposed or refused actions made.
- Make sure the LEA and the parents are on the same page about a child's IEP.

- Provide the parents with an opportunity to voice any concerns or suggestions.
- Provide sufficient information to ensure that the parent understands the rationale behind the LEA's decision regarding a proposed or refused action.
- Ensure that informed parental consent is obtained, as necessary.
- Assist the parent in determining the basis for any disagreements with proposed or refused actions addressed in the PWN, and whether to seek resolution of any dispute through local dispute resolution procedures, a state complaint, mediation, or a due process hearing.

When properly written, the PWN helps eliminate misunderstandings and doubts among the IEP team, and the length of the PWN depends on the circumstances triggering the document. With that being said, there are seven elements a PWN must include:[8]

- A description of the action proposed or refused by the LEA.
- An explanation of why the LEA proposes or refuses to take a specific action.
- A description of any other options the IEP team considered and the reasons for the rejection of those options.
- A description of each evaluation procedure, assessment, record, or report the LEA used as a basis for the proposed or refused action.
- A description of other factors that are relevant to the LEA's proposal or refusal.
- A statement that the parents of a child with a disability have protection under the procedural safeguards [for your state] and if the notice is not an initial referral for evaluation, the means by which a copy of the description of the procedural safeguards can be obtained.
- Sources for parents to contact in order to obtain assistance in understanding the provisions of the notice requirements.

A PWN must be written in language[9] that must be understandable to the general public, and it must be provided in the native language of the parents, or other mode of communication used by the parents. This means no special education jargon or acronyms. If the native[10] language or mode of communication used by the parents is not a written language, the LEA must take steps to ensure that the notice is translated orally or by other means to the parents in the native language or mode of communication, the parents understand the content of the notice, and that there is written evidence that the two previous requirements have been met.

The Office of Special Education Programs (OSEP) has further noted that a PWN's purpose is to ensure that a parent understands the proposed special education supports and services that the LEA will provide. Furthermore, the OSEP states that if a parent does not understand what is being proposed, the parent cannot have agreed to the proposed services. The PWN[11] has to be provided to the family within a reasonable amount of time before the LEA proposes or refuses:

- To initiate or change the identification, evaluation, or educational placement (including graduation with a standard or advanced diploma).
- The provision of a free appropriate public education (FAPE) for the child.

When it comes to "a reasonable amount of time" that the PWN must be sent prior to any changes made to an IEP, the U.S. Department of Education stated in 2006 that "[PWN] is provided in a wide variety of circumstances for which any one timeline would be too rigid, and, in many cases, might prove unworkable." Check with your school's special education department to see if they outline any such timelines for PWNs to be sent.

Here are some additional things to keep in mind when writing a PWN:

- With many regulations under the IDEA for IEPs, you are required to date the document or get documentation of consent. When it comes to PWN, the IDEA does not require the document to be dated. However, it is best practice to document when the notice was provided to the parent and, in some fashion, receive signed acknowledgment that the parent received the PWN. Let the parent know that the receipt does not constitute any agreement; rather, it is documentation on the LEA's part that the PWN was provided to the parent (because the LEA is the one who completes and writes up the PWN, not the parents).

- Some IEP systems will auto-generate a PWN for you. In other districts and states, you may need to type one up in a Word document. Federal and state regulations do not specify the PWN's format, so check with your administration on how they'd like it to be written up.
- Avoid cutting and pasting from previous IEPs or previously completed PWNs, and don't let a character limit stymie the length of your document. You can easily type up additional information in a Word document and attach it to the PWN.
- The PWN is required for every proposed or refused action related to a change in identification, evaluation, placement, or provision of FAPE—even if an IEP meeting was not held. So it is also important to make sure the parents understand that one PWN can serve multiple purposes, such as documenting initial eligibility, a FAPE decision, and placement.

As a professional on the IEP team, make sure that the family understands the difference between the PWN and a meeting notice. The meeting notice simply states that an IEP meeting is being held for a designated purpose (i.e., amendment or annual update). A PWN outlines every proposed or refused action discussed at the IEP meeting.

Manageable IEP Writing Tips

- Schedule uninterrupted time to write the IEP.
- Start early. Don't wait until the last minute because students deserve more than a last-minute IEP.

- Write the IEP as if the student will be switching schools next year; this is also called the *stranger test*. The IEP should be detailed enough that the student would have a relatively seamless transition to a new school.
- Know your student. Writing an IEP is a lot easier when you personally know and understand where the student is and how you would like to see them progress. The qualitative data is just as important as quantitative data.
- Be objective and use language that reflects measurable outcomes and goals. An IEP should be a clear picture of where the student is, what the student needs to be successful, and what the student will be working toward in the coming year.
- Check your spelling and grammar.
- Ask for help! If you're unsure, ask an administrator or colleague, or visit Mrs. D's VIPs Facebook group. Use your support system; you're not in this alone.

Summary

Writing an IEP takes time and collaboration. In the next chapter, you read about how to leverage the relationship with your general education teachers to help you with the IEP writing process.

Notes

1. https://sites.ed.gov/idea/regs/b/a/300.1
2. *Adapting Curriculum and Instruction in Inclusive Classrooms: A Teacher's Desk Reference,* by Deschenes, C., Ebeling, D., and Sprague, J., 1994.
3. https://sites.ed.gov/idea/regs/b/a/300.39
4. https://supreme.justia.com/cases/federal/us/468/883/
   https://www.law.cornell.edu/supremecourt/text/468/883

5. https://sites.ed.gov/idea/regs/b/b/300.160
   https://sites.ed.gov/idea/statute-chapter-33/subchapterii/1412/a/16
6. https://sites.ed.gov/idea/regs/b/a/300.43
7. https://sites.ed.gov/idea/regs/c/e/303.421
8. 34. C.F.R §300.503(b).
9. 34 C.F.R. §300.503(c)(1).
10. 34 C.F.R. §300.503(c)(2).
11. 34 C.F.R. §300.503(a).

Chapter 4

Increasing Team Participation at the IEP Meeting

Objective 1	Learner will discover multiple ways to collaborate with general education teachers throughout the IEP process.
Objective 2	Learner will implement the IEP Writing Timeline to facilitate active collaboration with the IEP team throughout the IEP meeting: before, during, and after.
Objective 3	Learner will be prepared for peer collaboration before, during, and after the IEP meeting.

Section 300.321(a) of the IDEA states that a general education teacher must be a part of every child's IEP team "if the child is, or may be, participating in the regular education environment."[1]

Recall from Chapter 1 who the members of a child's IEP team are, and more specifically, think about the child's general education teacher, or teachers. The general education teacher on a child's IEP team is the general education curriculum expert. This means that this professional can speak about the disabled child's peers in terms of what standards and skills are learned and expected in a specific grade level, and what content the child with an IEP will be introduced to in that classroom and grade level. With this knowledge, you are then able to discuss and make modifications and recommend accommodations together to best individualize instruction to ensure the student's progress and involvement in the general education curriculum and environment. In other words, you are not able to do your job as a special educator without the knowledge and expertise from your general education peer.

But to no fault of their own, what happens frequently is many general education teachers receive little to no special education training. Add to that, a classroom full of 30 students, 10 of which may have an IEP, 3 are on a 504 plan, and 6 are going through the referral process or are getting additional supports from that general education teacher without having an IEP. Teaching is not for the weary, and your general education peers are tough cookies—just like you! Which is why extending the olive branch to your peers, while also being mindful of their workloads, is so important in building positive rapport and strengthening your IEP teams.

In my experience, when I have been met with aversion to a child's IEP, the dislike or distrust comes from a place of misunderstanding or lack of understanding of special education and how it works—again, to no fault of the general education teacher. This makes our job as special education teachers more important because we get to train and educate our peers and build them up to feel like the true expert they are on the child's IEP team.

As you read through this chapter, remember that relationships take time to build and each team of professionals will have its own unique way of collaborating and communicating. There is no one right or wrong way, but there are some things you can do as the caseload manager to facilitate the bond.

Outside of the IEP Process

IEP team collaboration does not start and end with the IEP itself, and if you are to foster a truly collaborative IEP process with your general education peer, it begins within the walls of your school. It begins with an inclusive mind set (see Figure 4.1).

Fostering Inclusion

When you are facilitating inclusion in and out of the classroom, you want to make sure that you are facilitating actual inclusion. *Inclusion* is defined as "all students are presumed competent, welcomed as valued members of all general education classes and extra-curricular activities in their school, learning alongside their same aged peers and fully participating in the general education

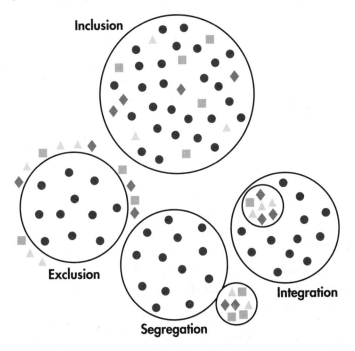

Figure 4.1 IEP Team Collaboration Begins with an Inclusive Mind Set.

instruction based on the general education curriculum, and are experiencing reciprocal social relationships." See Figure 4.2.

Numerous studies show positive effects of inclusion too, including:

- Higher expectations for student learning.
- Improved communication and social skills.
- More satisfying and diverse relationships.
- Improved outcomes in English language arts and mathematics.
- Better quality IEPs.
- Improved outcomes in education, employment, and independent living.

Differences

Mainstreaming	Inclusion
for students with disabilities	for all students, including gifted, neurotypical, and ESL students
improvement in social skills and academics	well-rounded students
modification support	team support + specialists
more about physical location of the student	more about including the student

Mainstreaming should always incorporate inclusion.

Figure 4.2 The Differences between Mainstreaming and Inclusion.

Co-Teaching Models

One of the most prevalent ways you will see inclusion happen in schools is through one or more models of co-teaching. Here are the six co-teaching models:

- **One Teach, One Observe:** One teacher teaches and the other teacher makes observations and takes data. This is a great option for one teacher to teach while the other provides additional learning support or behavioral supports.

- **One Teach, One Assist:** One teacher teaches and the other teacher assists and supports students.
- **Parallel Teaching:** Co-teachers divide the class in half and instruct students on the same material.
- **Station Teaching:** Co-teachers divide the class into small groups and instruct students at separate stations.
- **Alternative Teaching:** One teacher instructs students in a large group and the co-teacher instructs a smaller group of students on a specific topic of instruction. Also called "big/small group teaching."
- **Team Teaching:** Both teachers instruct and share the responsibilities of lead instruction with equally active roles in instruction. Also called "tag team teaching."

You can use more than one model at a time, switch models throughout the school week, or use one model with one co-teaching peer and another with a different co-teaching peer.

Co-teaching is one of those experiences that varies teacher to teacher, and I would guess that you have heard both sides of the story. I co-taught my very first year of teaching with two amazing middle school math teachers. For two periods in the morning, I would teach with one 7th-grade teacher, and two periods in the afternoon I'd be with a different 7th-grade math teacher. From the beginning of the school year, we communicated on the student needs in the classroom, and we asked questions and listened to one another about what our strengths were as educators and individuals, and how we could serve our students together.

For us, co-teaching looked like one teach, one observe and one teach, one assist most of the time. There were small moments throughout the day where we would team teach, and during study hall period, I would pull students on my caseload for small group instruction or to reteach skills. To share the planning workload, we would swap math units. I would teach one full unit for a week, and the next week or unit would be my co-teacher's responsibility to plan and teach. Again, this is what worked for us, and much of this planning and role-sharing was done through constant communication and collaboration.

Communication is key when it comes to co-teaching, just as it is with writing IEPs. To make any of the co-teaching models work for you and your co-teaching peer, you need to:

- Intentionally set aside time to collaborate. This could be during a planning period, weekly meetings, via email, through long-range grade-level planning, or using daily check-ins. Through communication you will find the most appropriate method for you.
- Plan who is doing what, including writing lesson plans, making copies, taking data, implementing supports, providing accommodations and modifications, and any additional responsibilities. There are some areas where your general education peer will shine and other areas where your special education expertise will shine.
- Read through and understand what it will take to implement each IEP and 504 plan in the classroom. I talk more about this in the next section.
- Determine and have agreed on expectations for students, including classroom rules and routines.
- Learn more about one another. What is each teacher's area of expertise, where do you each shine, and how can you complement the other teaching styles in the classroom?

How to Make the General Education Classroom More Inclusive

1. Have a desk for each student who participates in the classroom, even if only for a 30-minute period during the day. If students have bins, cubbies, or classroom lockers, special education students should also have the same. This goes for classroom workbooks and materials.

If students use a specific pencil or supply (e.g., utensil weights, lap pad, tilted book stand or slant board, wobble seat, visual schedule, core board), it is the responsibility of the special education teacher to make sure these supports are in the general education classroom setting too.

2. Anywhere there is a student list of names displayed or used, all student names should be on the list, even if a special education student only attends the classroom for a 30-minute period during the day. Examples include attendance boards, lunch count, reading lists, bulletin boards, classroom reward systems, and designated spots in a student line up.

3. Provide the disabled student with a peer buddy.

4. Set up a section of the classroom library with inclusive books about individuals with disabilities and differences. You can find a list of books here: www.mrsdscorner.com/60disabilitybooksforkids. Inclusion matters, and once you've built the framework for a truly inclusive school experience for your students with your peers, you've tackled more than half the battle of fostering a collaborative IEP writing process. Now you can get to writing those IEPs!

Pre-IEP Meeting: The IEP Writing Timeline's Alignment with Team Collaboration

Before you dive in to one of the most pivotal habits you may change or update in your IEP writing process, I recognize that you may feel very overwhelmed and maybe even uncomfortable with changes that you might need to make to your current IEP writing system. I want you to put your trust in me, let me guide you through it all, and know that baby steps are okay too.

Let me start by sharing a story about my own personal evolution as an IEP writer. I have been the teacher who scrambles to write IEPs the night before the IEP meeting. My first four years as a special education teacher, I never sent home a draft IEP or questionnaires to my fellow IEP team members. I fully embraced the special-education-island-of-one mentality, until I realized that special education was and is a team sport. That is when I developed the IEP Writing Timeline and became the teacher who wrote the Present Levels and goals two weeks prior to the meeting so I could send home the proposed draft IEP. What I have learned from my time teaching special education is that your habits and how you prioritize your job responsibilities affect your IEP writing process. This is how and why I developed the IEP Writing Timeline, and this moment is where it becomes your new IEP writing companion.

The IEP Writing Timeline (see Figure 4.3) is meant to help you manage the time and collaboration leading up to the child's IEP meeting. Having a structured timetable to abide by will help you narrow down when to do what, prioritize it by when, and make sure nothing slips through the cracks. Think of the IEP Writing Timeline as your living, breathing IEP to do list.

Districts and states across the country have different expectations and requirements for writing IEPs. My IEP Writing Timeline offers the big due dates with general time guidelines that you can further customize to meet the needs in your specific classroom. Be sure to check with your school's timeline policies before implementing it.

Also, recall that some states require IEP teams to send a proposed IEP draft prior to the IEP meeting. It will be beneficial for you to learn your school's policy on draft IEPs as well as your state's regulations.

Determining Dates and Sending Invites

Before you can implement the IEP Writing Timeline, you need to know who is on your caseload and what your due dates are. At the

IEP WRITING TIMELINE

45 days find common meeting times with IEP team members

30-45 days send invitation to parents; document attempts

30 days send input forms to IEP team members

14-30 days write the student's IEP

3-14 days send home proposed draft IEP (present levels + IEP goals)

1-7 days follow up on proposed draft with parents

5-7 days confirm IEP meeting with team: check room availability

1-3 days pre-IEP meeting or "staffing"

1 day print all documents needed for meeting

0 days hold IEP meeting

Next steps

The *Intentional* IEP

Figure 4.3   Refer to Chapter 1 for More Details on the IEP Writing Timeline.

beginning of the school year, when you receive your caseload list, and whenever you get a new-to-you student, you need to look at each IEP to determine that child's IEP due dates. Determining a child's IEP expiration date is your first step in creating a new habit, implementing it with fidelity, and starting off the IEP writing process on the right foot for each student on your caseload.

One of the most common IEP struggles is finding a common meeting time for all IEP team members, which is why I recommend starting 45 days out from the IEP meeting. You can then make sure that there are no upcoming staff development sessions, planned events like assemblies, school days off, or personal days for your professional peers on the IEP team in the week leading up to the child's IEP due date.

One way to get ahead of a scheduling fiasco is to send a virtual calendar invite to the general education teacher of the child's annual IEP due date on your digital calendar. This lets them know at the beginning of the year who in their classroom has IEPs and gives them a visual of when IEP meetings are going to be held.

Once you have determined the date, you will want to send out formal invitations to each IEP member. This should occur anywhere from 30 to 45 days out from that date. Formal invitations are often created within your school's chosen IEP software and can easily be edited and printed from within the software. If you're unsure how to send out an IEP meeting invitation, reach out to your administrator.

Getting Team Input

Once you've sent out the formal invitation, it is time to get team input on progress and current supports. You can get input from your general education teachers in multiple ways, but my favorite is by sending out a general education teacher input form 30 days out from the IEP meeting date. Give this input form to any general education teachers who service or teach the student (such as specials teachers). This two-page form is a form of collaboration and allows your general education peers to provide input and feedback on how the student is performing in the general education classroom with their current IEP supports.

Refer to the appendix of this book for a copy of my printable General Education Teacher Input Form. In the age of technology, you may find a digital form more practical than a printable form. You can find the digital input form at www.theintentionaliep.com.

Any input form you send out should ask team members for information on student strengths and areas of need, utilization of currently provided accommodations and modifications, behaviors and social skills, how and how often a student participates, any improvements or skill regressions noticed, and any specific accommodations the teacher recommends for this student in that classroom setting. This information helps provide a clear picture of the student in preferred and non-preferred classes, and it gives all teachers a voice in the IEP process.

Why send this form out 30 days before the IEP meeting? This gives the team member time to complete the form and return it to you without rushing. It also gives you sufficient time to send gentle reminders to complete the form, if needed, and meet with the general education teacher to ask questions. One of the most beneficial pieces of collaboration comes from asking these two short, but very important questions:

- What supports (accommodations or modifications) does the student need to be successful in your general education classroom?
- What supports (training, data sheets, assistance) do you need as the teacher to help the student be successful in your general education classroom?

When I started reframing my questions to allow my general education peers to reflect on their strengths in their classrooms, as teachers and as content experts, I found myself better able to help them help our students meet goals and succeed. This one mind set shift might be all it takes to get a hesitant team member on board and involved because it presents the IEP process, including implementation, as a team effort. It also gives you insight as to what strengths a teacher has and what potential teacher training may need to be written into the IEP.

For example, if a teacher is unsure of how to help a student reach their goals in the classroom, you can offer support and share what strategies you utilize in small groups that the teacher can reinforce in the classroom. This conversation leads you into a discussion about potential IEP goals. Based on the data in the present levels that you've already written, what skills does the student need to work on over the next year in alignment with the student's same-aged, neurotypical peers? Chapter 3 notes how the Present Levels leave breadcrumbs to what IEP goals should be written, and with the help of your general education peer, you can determine what IEP goals to write into the proposed draft IEP. Many times, general education teachers find out what the child's goals are at the meeting. This could lead to uncertainty or a lack of understanding of why certain IEP goals were chosen and why other skills were not made a priority.

As you are determining the proposed IEP goals, you can discuss if there was something in particular that was helpful or significant over the last school year for the student and for the teacher. In addition, you can ask what whole group accommodations the teacher may be providing to all students, or if there are any accommodations being provided outside of what was written into the child's previous IEP. It's important to know these small tidbits of information because if it's something that was working well we can continue these efforts, or discontinue them if it was something that wasn't working well. Was there a specific skill that the student struggled with, or was a previous IEP goal too ambitious because the skill required a prerequisite skill that the student does not yet have mastery of? These questions and conversations help you and your peer to analyze the data together to make data-driven decisions about what IEP goals should be proposed at the IEP meeting.

Types of IEP Meetings

Part of the collaborative IEP writing process is letting the team know what type of IEP meeting is coming up, especially if it is not an annual or reevaluation meeting.

- Eligibility Meeting.
- Initial IEP Meeting (and Initial Reviews).

- Annual IEP Meeting.
- Student-Led IEP Meeting.
- Amendment IEP Meeting (also called a Revision Meeting).
- Reevaluation Meeting.
- Discipline Review Meeting.
- Dismissal IEP Meeting.

Chapter 1 discusses the different IEP meeting types.

During this collaborative conversation, this is also the time to prep the general education teacher with information about any data, work samples, or grade level curriculum or content that they may need to bring to the IEP meeting. Some might want a checklist of what to bring or talking points or sentence starters for what to share with parents, and others may not need additional assistance to prep for the upcoming IEP meeting. Without asking, you won't know.

Building the Draft IEP

Once you have all of the team's feedback and you have analyzed the data together, you will enter it into the Present Levels and add in those proposed IEP goals before sending home the proposed draft IEP. Your draft IEP will include only the Present Levels and proposed IEP goals. Any more information than that and you are walking the very fine line of predetermination of services. If your IEP writing system does not allow you to print only certain sections, I recommend copying and pasting these two sections into a Word document that is clearly labeled "DRAFT IEP" on all pages. Make sure to not include any support or service pages from the current IEP in the draft that is sent home, as it will cause confusion. Then, two weeks to a minimum of three school days before the IEP meeting date, send home the proposed draft IEP to the student's family.

Before sending home a draft IEP, have a peer or admin read it over. Everyone makes mistakes, and it's better to catch them before sending anything home.

Remember, special education is a team effort, so 5–7 days out from the IEP meeting you will confirm the IEP meeting date with the team. You will schedule a room for the meeting (if it won't be held in your classroom), ensuring that the room's technology is available and in working condition to conduct the IEP meeting. Don't forget to make sure the physical arrangement of the meeting room is conducive to an effective meeting and that each member is a part of the table and has a seat.

IEP Meeting Cart: Your Mobile IEP Meeting on Wheels

Think about how most IEP meeting rooms are (that aren't your classroom). They're often in conference rooms that are stagnant and stale. They're uninviting and it can make the emotions in an IEP meeting unintentionally heightened. IEP Meeting Carts are a simple, effective way to have a mobile IEP meeting room on wheels while making sure the meeting space is inviting for all IEP team members.

The benefit to an IEP Cart is the ability to make the meeting room or space more inviting, while also having all of the IEP meeting supplies and necessary documents you'll need in one spot. The thought is to have one cart per building or school. If you have a larger school, with thousands of students, it may be beneficial to have two carts—or if you have multiple floor levels, maybe one per floor (depending on where the IEP meetings are held). The responsibility for maintaining the cart is that of the IEP teams . . . as IEP writing and successes are a team effort, so is the cart.

What can go on your IEP Meeting Cart?

- Projector or document camera.
- Acrylic frame (to put a picture of the student in for the meeting).
- Bluetooth printer with a laptop and extra copy paper.
- File organizers and extra file folders.
- Blue pens, highlighters, paperclips, stapler, and other office supplies.
- Tissues.
- Extra copies of the Parental Safeguards and any other forms or papers that are frequently referenced.

It's our job as educators to make parents feel heard and welcomed and to let them know that they are an important part of their child's team.

By creating a more inviting space for the entire IEP team, you are welcoming each IEP team member to the table. Those who feel welcomed are more likely to participate, and with IEPs, participation from all team members is vital!

Learn more and see additional images of my IEP meeting cart here: www.mrsdscorner.com/iep-meeting-cart/.

Sometimes it may be necessary to hold a pre-IEP meeting before the IEP meeting. This is not a meeting held where a team determines what it will or will not offer to the student. This is a meeting to discuss concerns, offer suggestions, or determine additional supports at school or within the community that may be helpful for the child. This pre-IEP meeting does include the parent.

What to Bring to the IEP Meeting

The day before the IEP meeting, print out all of the documents needed so that everything is ready to go for the meeting on the following day. I recommend doing this because technology is finicky, the printer may be out of ink all of a sudden, there's no more printer paper, your computer won't turn on, the IEP system is down . . . you name it and I can almost guarantee that you've had one of these scenarios happen to you before. It's better to be over-prepared, and you'll thank yourself the morning of the IEP meeting. The day before, you can also send an informal, friendly reminder to the team about the meeting tomorrow.

Professionals on the IEP team will want to gather these items to bring with to the IEP meeting:

- Meeting agenda.
- Students' IEP binder.
- Progress notes.
- Data.
- Work samples.
- Students' cumulative folder.
- IEP team input forms.
- Copies of the draft IEP.
- Any relevant or needed parts of the general education curriculum.

There are a few things you may want to gather before the IEP meeting to bring with you or make sure are in the meeting room already, including but not limited to:

- Candy, snacks, water (ask admin first!).
- Tissues.

- Blue pens.
- Sticky notes.
- Paperclips, binder clips, stapler.
- Highlighters.

All of this prep work and collaboration has led you to the big day, the IEP meeting day.

During the IEP Meeting

Your prep work has prepared you and your general education teacher for this meeting, but the teamwork and collaboration isn't over because now it's time to make data-driven decisions together.

Assigning Clear Roles

If you are facilitating the IEP meeting, it may be helpful to assign roles to IEP team members, as the IEP meeting will not run itself. Meeting roles help foster an inclusive experience of collaboration, boost meeting productivity, and allow all members to be actively engaged in the conversations and decision-making. Most IEP teams have roles assigned, but if you notice a role missing, make sure to assign the role before beginning. Roles may include, but are not limited to:

- **Note Taker or Recorder:** This role includes documentation of key action items and decisions, questions or concerns from team members, and any next steps or follow-ups that need to occur after the meeting. This person's role could look very different on each IEP team; for example: the note taker on one team may be unofficially taking notes to back up what is written in the Prior Written Notice (PWN), while another team's note taker may be taking official meeting notes that will be attached to the child's IEP. This is a role that needs to be clearly defined.
- **Time Keeper:** To be mindful of every team member's time and the slated timeframe of the IEP meeting, the time keeper keeps track of time efficiency and time limits set forth on the meeting agenda. Remember that IEP meetings are not mandated for a

specific time (i.e., 45 minutes or 60 minutes) and team members should be provided all the time needed to collaborate and make decisions. If the meeting begins to run out of time, the time keeper can suggest a second meeting or alert the team with gentle reminders of the time left in the current IEP meeting.

- **Leader or Facilitator:** This is generally the special education teacher or caseload manager, and this person facilitates the meeting by following the agenda and making sure the team knows the meeting objectives, leading the meeting, keeping the discussions on track, and writing. This role might also be split into two separate roles of one leader and one facilitator.

As you begin the IEP meeting, have everyone introduce themselves and share their role at the IEP table, including the general education teacher.

You can provide table name tags for each team member, so roles and names can be remembered and used correctly and respectfully throughout the IEP meeting.

Reviewing the IEP

Using your IEP meeting agenda, you will go through the IEP in sections. Because you have already met with your general education peer and prepped them prior to the meeting, they can interject throughout the meeting with their input and data. Allow them to go over the student's grades, what they are seeing in their classroom in terms of strengths, needs, behaviors, social skills, and so on, what accommodations are and aren't working, share any data and work samples they may have, and share information about that grade level's state and district testing. Remember, general education teachers are content level experts for the grade level they teach. This is their time to shine too!

Encourage team members to ask clarifying questions throughout the meeting. Clarifying questions will help the team understand what someone is saying, suggesting, or recommending by attempting to eliminate or prevent misunderstandings or ambiguity. These types of questions help all team members in making sure what was stated is properly understood, while potentially asking for more information or a clearer, more factual understanding of the topic.

Clarifying the Next Steps

As you round up the IEP meeting, remember to summarize any major points discussed, any agreements that were made, and any disagreements and how those will be documented in the child's IEP. Let the team know when to expect copies of the finalized IEP, if not provided at the IEP meeting, and let the general education teacher know that you will be checking in, in a couple of days, to talk about implementation and next steps.

IEP Team Member Attendance Excusal

One of the biggest questions about team attendance is excusal of other IEP team members from the meeting. How does that work? Here are two scenarios where it may be appropriate for an individual to not be present at an IEP meeting:

- A member of the child's IEP team may be excused from attending an IEP meeting if the member's area of the curriculum or service will not be discussed or modified and if the parent and school agree.
- An IEP team member may be excused if the member's area of curriculum or service will be discussed or modified, if the team member submits a written report to the parent and other members of the IEP team in advance, and if the parent provides written consent.

It is important to note that many courts focus attention on the requirement that the general education teacher attends the IEP meeting, finding that if the general education teacher is not present, the parents are ultimately denied the opportunity to participate meaningfully in the development of the IEP, which is a denial of FAPE.

> FAPE stands for Free Appropriate Public Education and emphasizes special education supports and services, preparing the child for "further education, employment, and independent living."

Section 1414(d)(1)(c) of the IDEA has this to say about excusal from an IEP meeting:[2]

- "(i) Attendance not necessary: A member of the IEP Team shall not be required to attend an IEP meeting, in whole or in part, if the parent of a child with a disability and the local educational agency agree that the attendance of such member is not necessary because the member's area of the curriculum or related services is not being modified or discussed in the meeting.
- (ii) Excusal: A member of the IEP Team may be excused from attending an IEP meeting, in whole or in part, when the meeting involves a modification to or discussion of the member's area of the curriculum or related services, if:
  - (I) the parent and the local educational agency consent to the excusal; and
  - (II) the member submits, in writing to the parent and the IEP Team, input into the development of the IEP prior to the meeting.
- (iii) Written agreement and consent required: A parent's agreement under clause (i) and consent under clause (ii) shall be in writing."

A guidance counselor cannot fulfill the role of a general education teacher at the IEP meeting.

After the IEP Meeting

Once you've finalized the child's IEP, you need to provide a copy to each person on the child's IEP team as well as any school professional who works with the student. When delivering the final printed copies of the IEP to team members, have the team members sign a piece of paper stating they received the final IEP for the child. This acts as a data point for you as the special education teacher as an acknowledgment and receipt of receiving the child's IEP. An example of this document is shown in the book's appendix.

In addition to handing out the finalized IEP to all of the child's team members at school, it will be beneficial to attach an IEP snapshot to the front of the child's IEP. This is often referred to as an *IEP at a glance,* and sometimes the IEP writing system you are using can generate one for you. An IEP snapshot should include the student's IEP goals and objectives, accommodations and modifications, student services, and possibly the student's schedule. Many general education teachers prefer for the IEP snapshot to be explained, rather than handed out. Carving out 15 to 30 minutes to discuss what is on the IEP snapshot and what this means for the general education teacher in terms of expectations and responsibilities helps you solidify the collaborative team approach.

Keeping Collaboration Front of Mind

This after-IEP meeting is not a "you have to do this because it's a legal document" conversation. Rather, it is a fluid and flexible conversation about realistic expectations and responsibilities. Covering topics like the difference between IEP goals and objectives, what order the IEP goals will be worked on, what the general education teacher needs to do to help the student, how to implement a specific accommodation for the student, what the goals and outcomes are, and what documentation the general education teacher needs to keep helps prevent future contentious collaboration.

If a student needs modifications to participate in the general education classroom and you will be providing the modifications (especially for testing), it is best to set timelines for when a general education teacher needs to provide you with the test. For example, if the student has a test on the United States' states and capitals next week and has a modification of lessened question responses, you could ask for the test to be provided to you a minimum of two school days before the test will be given. This gives you time to provide the modification with fidelity, while also respecting you as the specialist. However, if the general education teacher feels confident in providing the modification, asks for training on how to provide the modification to implement it on their own, or you will be in the classroom during the testing time, you may not need to set timelines.

Checking in throughout the Year

Throughout the school year, you will want to check in with your general education teacher. How this looks will be different for each IEP team, but remember that you don't want to check in to micromanage your peers, and letting them know that may go a long way in building rapport. You check in to make sure the supports and services the student is receiving are working, are being utilized, and to see if anyone on the IEP team needs anything. General education teachers are a vital part of the IEP Team. You cannot do your job effectively or efficiently without them, as they are the experts on the general education curriculum that you have to accommodate and modify. When asking a team member to do something, remind them that it's because you appreciate their input, you value their expertise, and you are inviting them to be a part of the student's education. Because they are a part of each child's education.

"People who feel appreciated will always do more than what's expected." —*Amy Rees Anderson*

General education teachers want to feel like valued members of the IEP team for the knowledge and expertise they bring to the table. When your team peers feel their input is valued and feel listened to and heard, the collaborative team approach to the IEP process is more likely to be successful. And when we work together as a team, it truly is the student who benefits from our collaboration.

Summary

You've learned a lot so far and I want you to remember this: where you are a year from now, or even a month from now, is a direct reflection of the choices you make today. And I am so proud of you for taking the steps in having a more streamlined, collaborative process for your IEP writing. Baby steps are okay, too! I am proud of you and am cheering you on.

Notes

1. https://sites.ed.gov/idea/regs/b/d/300.321/a
2. https://sites.ed.gov/idea/statute-chapter-33/subchapter-ii/1414/d/1/C

Chapter 5

Increasing Parent Participation in the IEP Process

Objective 1	Learner will discover multiple ways to collaborate with parents throughout the IEP process.
Objective 2	Learner will implement the IEP Writing Timeline to facilitate active collaboration.
Objective 3	Learner will be prepared for parent collaboration before, during, and after the IEP meeting.

Imagine you are going on a two-day hike without being told what gear to bring, what clothes or shoes to wear, where the hike will take you, or what the weather will be. On top of that, throw in that you don't have a guide or that your guide is coming along for the ride while you navigate, and this is your very first hike in your lifetime.

The day before the hike, all of the unknowns cause your emotions to scatter. You feel anxious, worried, excited, unprepared, yet hopeful all at the same time. You barely sleep or eat the night before because all you want to do is get the hike over with.

The day of the hike, you show up with a smile on your face, proud that you made it to the starting line, yet unknowingly very unprepared for the terrain you're about to experience. You find out that the hike is an expert level hike, and not even Google could have prepared you. Your guide had an emergency, so they left you a packet of what to and not to do, and then it started to rain. You are two miles into your hike and realize you didn't pack any waterproof gear, but you can't turn back now because you somehow maneuvered your way up the side of a rock wall. Plus turning back now would mean you gave up, and you can't do that.

Hopefully you get where this analogy is going. The hike you embarked on is the IEP meeting and you're the parent of the child with a disability.

A core principle of the federal IDEA law is the belief that parents are collaborative team members in the development of their child's IEP. IDEA was created for schools and parents to share equal responsibility in the IEP process, ensuring that the child's needs are met. And IDEA empowers parents and school professionals to work together to develop a shared vision of what the child's educational reality might be.

IEP meetings can be daunting, even to the most seasoned special needs parent, and even to veteran teachers. From nerves and anxiety, to exhaustion and a little bit of embarrassment, to tears of happiness for progress made and unity of the team. As special education teachers, professionals, and caseload managers, it is an important part of our job to prepare parents for the IEP meeting. In doing this, we create positive relationships and build rapport with the families we service.

The word *parent* means a lot of different things, and while family dynamics look different for every family—know that I will use the word *parent* to refer to the child's caregiver.

The purpose of the IEP meeting is to provide the parent and the student with their rights. For students, that means the development of an IEP that provides their Free Appropriate Public Education (FAPE) that also emphasizes special education supports and services, and prepares the child for "further education, employment, and independent living."[1] While the IDEA does not outline all scenarios that an IEP team may navigate through, it does outline a parent's participation, and parents have the right to participate in every decision related to the identification, evaluation, and placement of their child. What this means for parents is having the opportunity to participate meaningfully in the development of the student's IEP.[2] This means a lot of different things throughout the IEP process, and this chapter breaks down parent participation and team collaboration into three stages: pre-IEP meeting, the IEP meeting, and post-IEP meeting.

As the special education teacher, there are some things that you can do to be top-notch prepared for anything and ready to build that fully collaborative IEP experience for everyone on the team. As you read through this chapter, remember that when it comes to IEP team collaboration, relationships take time to build, and the same is true for a student's IEP team. Each family and team of professionals has a unique way of interacting and moving forward. There is no one right way to build positive rapport and strengthen a student's IEP team, but there are some things you can do to facilitate the bond.

The U.S. Supreme Court's decisions in these two landmark cases are evidence that the procedural right of collaboration between school personnel and a student's parents throughout the IEP process is vigorously protected by the courts: *Hendrick Hudson Central School District Board of Education v. Rowley* (1982) and *Endrew F. v. Douglas County School District* (2017). These cases emphasized the importance of the IEP writing collaboration, including during the planning stages, development of the IEP, and the implementation of services and supports.[3]

Pre-IEP Meeting

As discussed in Chapter 1, within Section 300.322 of IDEA,[4] parent participation is vital and the public agency (i.e., the school district) must take steps to ensure that the parent and child are aware of their rights and responsibilities as part of the IEP team. But when a parent arrives to your classroom with their child, whether at the beginning of the year or as a transfer mid-year, they come with their own set of IEP knowledge, and prior good and bad experiences. Many times the parent is looking for help, without knowing how to ask for help in this new and fresh experience. While it may not be your job to help parents unpack their past experiences and beliefs surrounding special education services, it is your job to support the parent through the process and provide them with any additional information and supports needed.

We all come with our own baggage in one form or another. We all have good and bad experiences that have shaped the person, the teacher, whom we are today. Keeping this information handy in the back of your mind, while also showing the family grace, can help you help the family, and ultimately build a strong bond that will withstand the tests of the school year.

Communication is a key part in making collaboration work, to the point that you can find the word "labor" within the word collaboration. You know that IEP progress reporting is outlined in a child's IEP, but that's not when communication starts and ends.

Open communication throughout the school year will help you build stronger relationships, and what works for one family may or may not work for another family.

Reaching Out to the Family

On or before the first day you have a child with a disability in your classroom, it is best practice to reach out to the family as a point of contact for them, and also as a support system for them. With technology at your fingertips, this can be accomplished through a phone call, an email, a text message, or a communication app. Many times, you'll find out that a parent is sailing through these uncharted waters alone, but you as the special education teacher possess a very particular set of professional skills and have a sense of what they're feeling and going through. Calling the parent to let them know they are not alone in the process puts your best foot forward and shows the parent you care.

You may even be in a scenario where the parent reaches out to you first! My first year teaching in a self-contained classroom setting, I vividly remember having to go to meet-the-teacher night and none of my parents showing up. But I did get a call from the office that one of my student's parents had left something for me. It was a welcome to the classroom gift (a teacher's survival kit with many teacher essentials inside it) and a three-ring binder that served as the child's Bible. Inside this binder were beautiful pictures of the child growing up, things this child loved to do and eat, information about the child's disabilities and how these affected this student, and also family information. This was my fifth year teaching, but only the first time I had ever received such a welcome from a family. This experience taught me that a new teacher is a fresh start for this family, and we were going work together, through the good and bad, to make our classroom a home—not only for this child, but for all of my students and families. Sometimes a phone call or small token of appreciation can go a long way. This is true for the families you service as well.

Before the IEP meeting is a crucial part of the special education process. There is a lot happening behind the scenes that you are preparing and writing that a parent may not be aware of. Whether it is an eligibility, initial, or annual IEP meeting, or a reevaluation meeting, you can use the IEP Writing Timeline to help you keep the family involved in the process. As Chapter 1 notes, the IEP Writing Timeline is based on best practices, but that it is also fluid and flexible. Figure 5.1 shows the IEP Writing Timeline again.

Seeking Information from the Parents

Before an IEP meeting, asking the parents about the following will provide you with a lot of valuable data for the Present Levels section of the child's IEP:

- Ask the parent about the child's likes, dislikes, strengths, needs, and everything in between. A lot of the time, you can use this information to your advantage when lesson planning, when trying to get the student to participate in a non-preferred task, and when choosing the most appropriate accommodations and modifications.
- Ask the parent what they hope their child accomplishes over the next calendar year, and what skills, if any, they want to prioritize. While we can't possibly work on all of the skills in a single school year, we can work together to choose a maximum of three or four skills to prioritize this school year, and make a note of the others in the Present Levels and meeting minutes, as necessary. You can then align the prioritized skills with what IEP goals are written.
- Ask the parent to share what supports, interventions, and activities have been effective or ineffective over the last year. This may include what's working at home.
- Ask the parent about what, if any, outside services the child participates in. This might include ABA therapy, occupational therapy, physical therapy, horseback riding, or something else. While you are not permitted to reach out to the outside service providers without parental consent, making a note of the outside services in the child's IEP is a beneficial data point.

- Ask the parent to make a list of things that were helpful or significant over the last year, and maybe you do this together. You can also do this at the end of a school year to provide a bridge of what worked and didn't work from one teacher or school to the next.

A lot of this information can be shared through what I call a Parent Input Form (also known as a questionnaire). This is step three of the IEP Writing Timeline and is sent out to the parent 30 days prior to the IEP meeting.

Refer to the appendix of this book for a copy of my printable Parent Input Form. In the age of technology, you may find a digital form more practical than a printable form. You can find the digital input form at www.theintentionaliep.com.

The information that you gather from the parent input forms and the general education and paraprofessional input forms will help you craft the most accurate Present Levels. As is discussed in Chapter 3, the data in the Present Levels section will leave breadcrumbs throughout the rest of the IEP and guide you into what IEP goals should be worked on next. The Present Levels and IEP Goals sections make up your proposed draft IEP, which should be sent home to the parent anywhere from 3 days to 14 days before the IEP meeting, according to the IEP Writing Timeline.

Some states do require IEP teams to send a proposed IEP draft prior to the IEP meeting. It will be beneficial for you to learn your school's policy on draft IEPs as well as your state's regulations.

Sending the Draft IEP Home

When sending home the proposed draft IEP, you want to make sure the parent knows:

- The proposed draft is just that, a draft, and not the final IEP.
- Anything in it can be changed at any time.
- How the proposed IEP goals were chosen.

> Remind parents that not all skills and progress will show up immediately. Try to help parents understand the smaller steps the child is making toward the bigger goals.

By sending the proposed draft IEP a minimum of three school days in advance, you are giving the parent enough time to read and digest the data and the suggestions for IEP goals. Draft IEPs level the playing field and give parents the same information going into the IEP meeting that the team of professionals has. You're also giving the parent enough time to determine any concerns or suggestions they may have before you reach out and follow up, or hold the IEP meeting.

When sending home the proposed draft, add a personal touch. You can do this by putting a sticky note on the front that says something like, "I'm looking forward to meeting with you [insert parent's names]. I want to show you the great work [student's name] has been doing! Don't forget to reach out if you have any questions."

Helping Parents Prepare

Chapter 1 notes the many different types of IEP meetings. Depending on the type of IEP meeting coming up, you may find it beneficial to reach out to the family to tell parents what to expect during the meeting, as well as informing them of how they can participate in the IEP meeting itself (i.e., sharing information, assisting with the development of IEP goals, assisting in the determination of related services, and providing or not providing consent for services and supports). Here are a few ideas on how you can help parents prepare for an upcoming IEP meeting.

- **Prepare parents for the wait.** Nothing happens overnight, and some IDEA and state timelines are long. As the special education teacher, you may find it helpful to suggest things for parents to do that will help them through the waiting time. This might include introducing parents to outside resources, community resources, other parents, agencies, reading materials, and so on, that may be relevant to understanding their child and what their child may need. It's also helpful to explain calendar days versus school days.

A *calendar day* is any day on the calendar, regardless of weekend or weekday. This includes holidays and weekends. A *school day* is any day that your school or district is in session. A *business day* is any weekday, not including holiday or weekends. Typically, one business day is equivalent to two calendar days.

- **Ask how much information they want to receive.** What makes each IEP team so unique is the human beings who make up the team. This includes similarities, but also differences in how we process information, what information we like or need to have, how much information is too much, what our unique learning styles are, and when we want or need access to this information. Ask parents these clarifying questions. Do they like having all of the information on overload, or do they need it chunked into smaller, more digestible tidbits?
- One of my favorite ways to do this is with a slider scale. On a scale of 1 to 5, 1 being "don't tell me anything" and 5 being "I want all the information right now," how would you answer this question . . .

- **Remind parents.** Remind them that they did the right thing by bringing their child in for an evaluation, and also remind parents that it is okay to not understand every detail, every report, or every choice or option immediately. It is okay to need space and time to feel, think, question, take in new information, and walk with grace through this process. And most of all, remind parents to trust themselves and what they know about their child. Don't let a parent dismiss or underestimate their knowledge of their own child! They are the expert.
- **Let parents know they can ask questions.** Ask, ask, ask! Their questions are important, and you need them to let you know what they need to be fully involved in the IEP process. But also remember to slow down and give the parents time to process and think about any questions they may have. All of the upcoming information will be new and more than likely include unfamiliar jargon. It's overwhelming, and you don't want to add to their feeling of being overwhelmed if you can help it.
- **Let parents know what to bring with them to the upcoming meeting, and let them know what to expect and what topics they should be prepared to talk about.** Tell them they can—and are encouraged to—bring a list of thoughts, questions, and/or expectations they want to discuss at the meeting.

While these are not requirements under any federal or state regulations, these are best practices. And while you don't have to implement all of these ideas, starting with one or two and building from there will help you build that collaborative IEP team.

During the IEP Meeting

IEP meetings should be on a mutually agreed on date and time, and scheduled a minimum of 30 to 45 days before the IEP meeting—per the IEP Writing Timeline.[5] This gives everyone on the IEP team time to prepare for the meeting, and the parent enough time to provide input and look over the proposed draft IEP. (Refer to Chapter 1 for the types of IEP meetings.)

Parent Attendance

In the best case scenario, you would have all of your students' parents attend their meetings. You would hear back from them about their attendance, they would be actively involved, and the world would keep gloriously turning. But in the real world, parents are busy. And sometimes it is difficult to get in contact with them. But you do know that the parent of a child with a disability must be invited to any upcoming IEP meeting, regardless of the type of IEP meeting, and Section 300.322 of the IDEA says this about the Public Agency's responsibility:

"(a) Each public agency must take steps to ensure that one or both of the parents of a child with a disability are present at each IEP Team meeting or are afforded the opportunity to participate, including:

- Notifying parents of the meeting early enough to ensure that they will have an opportunity to attend; and
- Scheduling the meeting at a mutually agreed on time and place."[6]

Per best practices, you should begin sending out the IEP meeting invitations 30–45 days prior to the IEP meeting. When a parent is unreachable or is not responding to meeting invites, you need to make sure you have a minimum of three documented, separate attempts to invite the parent to the IEP meeting. I recommend using different communication methods, but making sure each attempt is dated and documented correctly. Yes, you have the official invitations from your IEP writing system that should be printed and dated and sent home. But you can also:

- Contact the family via phone.
- Email the parent a copy of the invitation with "Read Receipt" on it.
- Email the parent a copy through DocuSign or a similar web app.
- Have someone else from the IEP team reach out.
- Make a home visit.

Best practice is to wait two to three business or school days before documenting a second attempt, but check with your school, as it may have its own policy for this situation.

No matter which communication method you choose, it may be beneficial to mention in your message to the parent that under Section 300.328, "the parent of a child with a disability and a public agency may agree to use alternative means of meeting participation, such as video conferences and conference calls." This means parents do not physically need to be in attendance of an IEP meeting, and that you can use a phone conference with the IEP team as attendance or attendance via Zoom, for example.

If you are unsuccessful in reaching the parent for scheduling the IEP meeting, you are permitted under the IDEA law to hold the IEP meeting without the parent present. It is best practice to still let the parent know where and when the IEP meeting will be held.

If the child is a ward of the state or the parents cannot be located, the public agency must appoint a surrogate parent, outlined in Section 300.45. In the case of a child who is a ward of the state, the student's parents must be given the opportunity to participate, unless the parent's rights that oversee education have been severed by the court.

Parent Absences

This brings me to the topic of parent absences at an IEP meeting. As an educator, you work with a lot of families. Some parents will be at every IEP meeting and check in frequently, while others will appear more absent. In the latter case, it's important to realize that some parents may not understand the importance of their attendance or involvement in the IEP process for their child, or that you—the professional—value their input and want to work collaboratively together with them. But there may also be other reasons why a parent does not show up to an IEP meeting, and as a special education teacher it is important that you consider all of the options before making judgments.

There are a lot of reasons that a parent may not want to or be able to attend an IEP meeting. It is not your place as the educator to judge, but rather extend grace and offer supports as best you can. Here are a few reasons that parents may not seem like active participants in the IEP process, even though they truly are trying their best:

- The parent may have forgotten about the IEP meeting. This happens to the best of us!
- The parent may not be able to get out of work, find child care for the student's siblings, or have a conflict with something else on their schedule.
- The parent may not have transportation, or may be reluctant to drive in the current weather conditions. The parent may also be stuck in traffic.
- The parent may have triggering PTSD from personal experiences in school.
- The parent may have a disability and may be unsure or afraid to ask for assistance through the process.
- The parent may be sick or be caring for another sick individual.
- The parent might have a last-minute emergency.
- The parent may be intimidated by the process or worried about the outcome.
- The parent may have communication difficulties and is anticipating frustration and overwhelm.
- The parent may not feel like they have appropriate clothing for the meeting.
- The parent may not realize the importance of their participation in the IEP process and the value of their input.

How a parent participates in their child's IEP process will look very different, parent to parent, and situation to situation. Again, it is not your place to judge; rather, it is your job to offer supports and extend grace in all situations.

I once worked with a parent whose child was in my 5th-grade resource classroom. This parent was not able to attend any IEP meetings due to work; rather, we would have phone conversations about changes or updates and the parent would agree via phone. This parent was very supportive of the IEP process and was able to be an active participant in her own way, which was still very valuable to the IEP process, the IEP team, and the student.

It's also very important to remember as professionals that just because there is no response from a parent does not mean that the parent is absent or does not care. While it is true that not all families are comfortable having a relationship with school professionals, or they come to you with heavy and delicate previous experiences, it is important that you resist labeling parents and are respectful of each family's choices.

Before the IEP Meeting Starts

Remember how scary and overwhelming IEP meetings can be to parents. To encourage and support parents' participation and comfort with the IEP meeting, keep these points in mind:

- Meet parents in the office and walk with them to the meeting place. You can also let them know where the restrooms are located and offer them a few minutes to use the restrooms before the meeting begins.
- When you arrive in the meeting room, make sure everyone is part of the table. No one should be sitting on the outskirts of the room. Together, you are the IEP team.
- Place a "Meeting in Progress" sign on the door of the meeting room to hopefully avoid any potential interruptions. This is especially important if the meeting is being held in a common room.
- If a parent is late to the IEP meeting, give the parents a call. Even if you think a parent is not going to attend the meeting, use an understanding tone of voice and say something like, "Hey [insert parent name], this is [insert your name] and I'm calling to see if you are available for today's IEP meeting, if you need to reschedule, or are having trouble getting here? We just want

to be sure that everything is okay! We hope to hear from you soon." You can also remind the parent that they can video conference in if needed. Even if the parent does not respond, you are doing your due diligence as an IEP team member at including the parent in the IEP process.

- Have an agenda printed and ready to go. Have a copy available for each meeting attendee or have the agenda in a place where every attendee can see it. You can also state the timeframe of the meeting (i.e., 30 minutes, 45 minutes), so everyone stays on track. However, know that legally if an IEP takes longer than the accounted for time, the IEP team cannot rush a parent through the meeting. Parents have rights, and it is our job to make sure a parent understands what is in their child's IEP, what it means, and everything in between. If you find that you've run out of time, schedule a second meeting.
- Tab parts of the printed IEP so you can easily find them. It may, also, be a wise choice to put tabs where you will want parents to sign. This helps so you don't miss any sections or spots too, and everything gets covered.

Starting the IEP Meeting

The IEP meeting is here and it's go time! The best way to start an IEP meeting with parent collaboration in mind is to start with a welcome message that includes a thank you to all team members for being present, active members throughout the process . . . especially the parents! You might also want to have a picture of the student present and in view of the team. You can also begin the conversation with a story or two of what the child does well or what you enjoy about having the child in your classroom.

After a short welcome, you will want to state the reason for today's IEP meeting, and it may also be helpful to let the parent know that they have a right to request more time or another IEP meeting.

Then have everyone introduce themselves and their role in the child's education. For example, "Hi! My name is Stephanie and I am the child's special education teacher and caseload manager."

Student self-advocacy is such an important life skill, and this may be a great opportunity to have the child be a part of the IEP meeting (yes, even before transition age!). At any age, it is possible. The student could say the welcome message, you could show a recording of the child performing a task in the classroom or sharing about their likes or strengths, or any other number of things.

Tips for Going through the IEP with Families

It is important to go through the IEP page by page, in numerical order, and showcase it this way on the meeting agenda as well. Become familiar with your school's or state's IEP format, as most IEP formats build on each other, and each section is showcased in a way that allows for the next section to be built on the previous section. It's best to avoid skipping around to prevent confusion or additional overwhelm, and to prevent a section from being missed in discussion.

If there are new evaluation or diagnostic test results, or other new data to share and analyze:

- Go slowly when explaining new results and explain each score's significance. All of the numbers may be super confusing, so try to use concrete examples as much as possible. Remember that one member of the IEP team must be able to "interpret the instructional implications of evaluation results."[7]
- Remind parents that test scores are only one way of understanding the child and their child's learning. There are many other ways to learn about a child's abilities, and remind parents

that this is why their input is so valuable. You can also suggest to the parent that they reread the reports when they get home. It doesn't have to be reviewed immediately, they can take their time.

- Clarify that a label or eligibility classification does not indicate what services are supports their child may need. Remind parents that their child is still the same unique, wonderful child they were before the evaluations and eligibility. It may also be helpful to remind parents that their child does not need to be cured or fixed. Their child simply needs supports. A new label or evaluation result will not lower the child's expectations, and the evaluations are part of the formal IEP process. This also doesn't mean that we view the child as the label—however, this is a step we must take together to get the child the right supports.

Avoid Jargon

When going through each section of the IEP, have the team do their best to avoid acronyms and jargon. Compare this situation to sitting in a doctor's office and the doctor saying you need to begin taking these five prescriptions daily. You have no idea what they are, what the side effects might be, when or how to take them, but you trust your doctor. This is comparable to how parents feel when you talk in special education alphabet soup lingo. It might be a good idea to have a list of acronyms available and handy for parents and other team members.

As you work through each section of the IEP, if you have a student work sample or raw data to share, share it! Parents want to see their child's work, and they want to know what the data is. This leads to more fruitful, data-driven decisions at your IEP meetings.

Seek Feedback from Parents

One thing I have learned from working with parents is how appreciative parents are when asked for their input. So as you work through the IEP, take a moment after each IEP section to ask parents, "what questions or concerns do you have?" In these moments, make sure you are listening to what the parent is saying and that you are validating their concerns. You can be very well intentioned, yet be unknowingly pushing parents to share information they may not feel comfortable sharing, or not yet want to share. Cast the serve and leave the ball in their court. It may also be helpful to ask parents if they need a short break.

Take Breaks If Things Get Emotionally Charged

Speaking of needing a break during an IEP meeting, it is okay to request a break at any time, especially if the meeting becomes emotionally charged. I have been in IEP meetings where parents cry, and I have been the one in an IEP meeting crying. I've also been in IEP meetings where a team member was very angry, and what I will say about anger showing up is that anger, or any other strong emotion, is born out of love. There are often many other underlying factors, but anger is a sign that patience and communication are needed in that moment. Listening and open communication will often alleviate much of the anger, but you also need to make sure that you are discussing issues before they become problems, and that you are resolving problems before they result in conflict.

Emotions are almost a given at IEP meetings, good and bad. And as mentioned, there are often other underlying factors that are aiding the bubbling emotions to overflow. Past events or additional concerns not related to the topic of the IEP meeting may be brought up, and while I do not recommend ignoring them, this is the time to make a note of the topics and revisit them. At the end of the meeting, you can quickly recap any topics that need to be revisited and how those topics will be dealt with.

Summarize the Main Points

As you round up the IEP meeting, you will want to summarize any major points discussed and any agreements that were made. It will also be beneficial to bring up any disagreements that were made and how those will be documented in the Prior Written Notice (PWN) and meeting minutes.

Getting Parental Consent

Before the parent signs, or does not sign, the IEP, briefly summarize what was discussed during the IEP meeting. If a parent consents to the IEP as it was discussed and written at the IEP meeting, the parent will sign the document and the new IEP will be implemented immediately. If a parent does not consent to the IEP and does not sign the IEP, the school is not permitted to implement the IEP as it was discussed and written during the meeting. However, the school can still implement the IEP after submitting to the parent in writing to let them know of intent to implement the IEP. The school must wait 14 days to implement the IEP then.

Let me restate this in a different way: The IDEA law does not require a child's parent to sign the IEP. Parents are required to give informed consent before the school can provide services in the initial IEP, but not subsequent IEPs. However, some states do include a provision for parents to sign and others require written consent, so it's important to check with and refer to your state's regulations.

A parent signing the attendance page of the IEP does not provide consent or approval on their behalf. If a parent is reluctant to sign the meeting attendance page, remind them that attendance at the meeting is not an approval or denial of services.

After the IEP Meeting

You've successfully written the IEP and held the IEP meeting, but your collaboration duty is only beginning. The afternoon after the IEP meeting, or the morning after, send the parent an email and thank them for coming to the IEP meeting and participating in the process. You can also let them know you'll be sending home the final IEP on a specific date, and that you'll call in a few days to check in.

Within a day, and no more than 48 hours, you will want to send home the finalized IEP to the family. Typically this looks like a printed copy of the IEP that is sent home in the child's backpack, but it is best practice to ask your school admin how they prefer finalized IEPs to be delivered.

Handling Disputes from Parents

Let's say that the parent disagrees with a decision made by the IEP team. What happens next? The parent may initiate and go through what is called due process. This must be filed within two years of when the disagreement occurred. Each party's rights can be found in Section 300.512.

When the public agency receives the due process hearing request, they have 10 days to respond. If the school does not believe the request has all the needed or required information, and an agreement has not been made, it has 15 days to inform the hearing officer that they believe the request is deficient. The school must also schedule a dispute resolution meeting within 15 calendar days of receiving the request for a due process hearing.

From there, the hearing officer has five days to determine if the complaint meets all of the requirements. Each public agency must keep a list of people who serve as hearing officers. The list must include a statement of the qualifications of each of these people.

Here are the hearing officer requirements per the IDEA, Section 300.511:

- The hearing officer must not be an employee of the SEA or the LEA involved in the education or care of the child.
- The hearing officer must not have a personal or professional interest that conflicts with their objectivity in the hearing.
- The hearing officer must have knowledge of, and the ability to understand, IDEA's provisions, federal and state regulations pertaining to IDEA, and legal interpretations of IDEA made by federal and state courts.
- The hearing officer must have the knowledge and ability to conduct hearings in keeping with appropriate, standard legal practice.
- The hearing officer must have the knowledge and ability to render and write decisions in keeping with appropriate, standard legal practice.

If the hearing officer determines the complaint does not provide enough information, the school can agree to let the parent add more information or the hearing officer can allow more information to be included. This needs to be done at least 5 days before the hearing is scheduled.

At the dispute resolution meeting, if a resolution is reached, the school has 30 days to implement any changes. If a resolution is not met, the hearing must be held within 30 days.

At least 5 days before the hearing, both sides must give all evaluations to the other including any recommendations

(continued)

(continued)

provided. This means the school must provide any information, data, and evaluations to the family and vice versa. If this information is not provided, it cannot be provided at the hearing. In turn, this information cannot be used in the hearing.

Once the hearing is over, the hearing officer has 30 days to provide a written decision. This timeline can be extended as well. The final decision is reached not later than 45 days after the 30-day resolution period expires. You can read more about hearing decisions in Section 300.513.

If a parent or the public agency does not agree to the hearing officer's decision, they may file an appeal with the State court within 90 days of the hearing officer's decision. This is done through what is called civil action.

Remember that all of the information about parents' and students' rights is further outlined in the Procedural Safeguards.

A day or two after sending home the finalized IEP, giving the family time to mentally recover and dissect how the meeting went, give the family a friendly call. Check in to show you care, because you do care, and let the parent know that your collaboration doesn't stop at the end of the IEP meeting. See if they have any additional questions and let them know that you truly are there for them and their child. Ask if they need anything additionally clarified or explained, or if they've changed their mind about a specific service or support and would like to amend anything. You can also remind them that amendments can happen at any time!

In addition to this, don't forget to take care of any other business that was brought up at the IEP meeting. Maybe you need to connect the family with a community service for transition, or maybe the family wants a copy of the child's school file. Don't forget to follow up with all of the non-IEP stuff too.

Summary

To close out this chapter, remember: meetings are a part of any teacher's life, and it is important that you don't just wing it. Be prepared and keep a positive mind set. You've got this! And always remember that each year is different, and every IEP meeting is different. Don't let one downhill meeting break you.

Notes

1. https://sites.ed.gov/idea/about-idea/#IDEA-Purpose
2. https://sites.ed.gov/idea/regs/b/d/300.322
3. https://iris.peabody.vanderbilt.edu/wp-content/uploads/pdf_info_briefs/iep_process_common_errors_information_brief.pdf#:~:text=A%20procedural%20error%20that%20may,(1982)%20and%20Endrew%20F.
4. https://sites.ed.gov/idea/regs/b/d/300.322
5. law.cornell.edu/cfr/text/34/300.324
6. https://sites.ed.gov/idea/regs/b/d/300.322
7. https://sites.ed.gov/idea/regs/b/d/300.321

Outro/Conclusion

Passing the Baton to You!

IEP writing can be a very daunting task when you sit back and think about all of the variables that go into a student's IEP process. An IEP is so much more than a couple of pieces of paper, and my hope is that by reaching the end of this book you see the connection among all of the living parts of an IEP. Because when you realize the connection between all of the moving parts, that's when the magic happens.

You get to change students' lives. You get to change families' lives. Your influence lasts far more than one calendar year, or however long a student is in your classroom. That is the power you hold for each student that passes through your classroom every single day. As a special education teacher, this influence is even more powerful because of the IEPs you write. You have the power to build students up or tear them down. You can be a solution seeker or a "just pass them" through-er. You can stand strong in your advocacy and fight for the services your students so rightfully deserve and need, or let another student fall through the cracks. Which side of education will you stand on? I sure hope it's with me and hundreds of thousands of other teachers, parents, students, advocates, administrators, paraprofessionals . . . because the work that you are doing matters.

Use the knowledge you've learned in this book to empower your teacher soul, even the part of your teacher soul that doesn't like writing IEPs. You have the necessary tools to make it happen, to write IEPs more effectively and efficiently. It all comes back to your habits and the habits that are passed on to you. Do your current habits align with collaborative IEP writing? Your last step is to use the free space on the next page to identify what successful collaborative IEP writing looks like for your IEP teams, and note what potential barriers you foresee. Start open dialogue with your colleagues about what you've learned in this book, and how you, together as a team, can implement some of the new strategies you've learned.

I am here for you every step of the way. Your days of IEPing alone are over, and know that I am here cheering on you and your students! Keep up the great work; you're doing an amazing job.

Appendix:
Helpful Templates

Progress Monitoring
3x5 Notecard

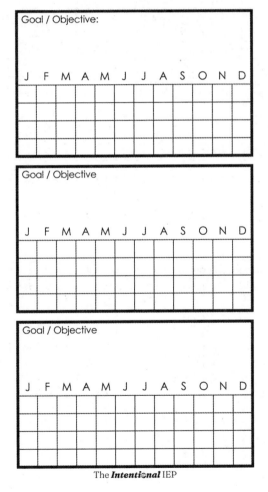

Goal / Objective:

J F M A M J J A S O N D

Goal / Objective

J F M A M J J A S O N D

Goal / Objective

J F M A M J J A S O N D

General Ed IEP Questionnaire   Side A

Child's Name: _____   Class: _____   Grade: _____
Teacher: _____

As **[insert child's name]**'s caseload manager, it is my responsibility to ensure that this student's IEP is appropriate and being followed. Please assist me in monitoring the progress of this student by filling out this form, attaching any work samples, and returning it to me by **[insert date]**. Thank you!

	Never		Sometimes		Always
Comes to class prepared.	1	2	3	4	5
Follows classroom rules and routines.	1	2	3	4	5
Compliant and follows directions.	1	2	3	4	5
Participates appropriately in class.	1	2	3	4	5
Adjusts readily to change.	1	2	3	4	5
Remains seated and is attentive.	1	2	3	4	5
Keeps hands, feet, and objects to self.	1	2	3	4	5
Completes assignments.	1	2	3	4	5
Interacts appropriately with peers.	1	2	3	4	5
Disruptive during classroom activities.	1	2	3	4	5
Shows an interest in learning.	1	2	3	4	5

What improvements have you noticed since the beginning of the school year?

What specific accommodations do you recommend for this student?

How does the student compare to grade level peers in each of these areas?

English / Language Arts	Mathematics	Science / Social Studies
Self-Help / Life Skills	Communication	Social Skills / Behavior

The *Intentional* IEP

IEP Meeting Checklist for General Ed Teachers

What should you bring to an IEP meeting?

o Student work samples from time in your classroom
o Any data you have taken on the student
o Current grades and performance data
o Notes on any interventions or supports you've provided
o Any additional requested documents
o A positive, collaborative attitude, and a willingness to ask for support if needed.
o Suggestion and solutions

Suggested Talking Points

- Glows and Grows – how has the student grown since being in your class? What strengths does the student possess?
- Share stories about having the child in your classroom.
- Share any interventions, strategies, or supports that you have already tried, and if they have been successful or not.
- Ask what something means if you are unsure. For example: if you hear an acronym you don't know, ask what it stands for and means. Asking for clarification can other team members at the meeting as well.
- Ask for team feedback on your role as the general education teacher, and as a key implementor of the child's IEP.
- Speak up if you don't agree with something, and have data to back up your opinions.
- What is the best method of communication for the family to reach you?

Potential Questions to Ask

- Who is responsible for implementing this support/service? How often? Where? When?
- Who is responsible for collecting data on this? How often? Where? When?
- What should we do if _____?
- How can I help support you (the parent) at home?

IEP Acknowledgement Receipt

Student Name: School Year:

IEP Start + End Date: School:

> By signing my name on this document, I acknowledge that I have received the student's IEP for this school year and that I will do my due diligence to familiarize myself with the student's IEP.

_____   _____
signature   signature

_____   _____   _____   _____
position   date   position   date

_____   _____
signature   signature

_____   _____   _____   _____
position   date   position   date

_____   _____
signature   signature

_____   _____   _____   _____
position   date   position   date

_____   _____
signature   signature

_____   _____   _____   _____
position   date   position   date

_____   _____
signature   signature

_____   _____   _____   _____
position   date   position   date

Parent Questionnaire

Side A

Child's Name: _____   DOB: _____   Grade: _____
Teacher: _____   Case Manager: _____

What do you hope your child accomplishes/learns over the next calendar year?

Please circle any 3 of the items below that you consider to be a top priority for next year.

Academics	Self-Help (toileting, feeding, dressing)	Mobility (walking)
Social / Behavioral	Executive Functioning (emotional regulation, problem solving, organization)	
Fine / Gross Motor	Communication / Language	Other:

Do you have any IEP goal recommendations for your child's upcoming IEP?

English / Language Arts	Mathematics	Science / Social Studies
Self-Help / Life Skills	Communication	Social Skills / Behavior

---

What are your long term life goals for your child?

Is there anything at home that your child needs assistance with? (skills, routines, etc.)

Would you like to receive more information on parent or in-home training at the IEP meeting?   Y   N

Would you like more information on community resources or services available?   Y   N

The *Intentional* IEP

Index